30, 60,
Hundredfold

Your Financial Harvest Released

30, 60,
Hundredfold

Your Financial Harvest Released

by

John Avanzini

Harrison House
Tulsa, Oklahoma

Unless otherwise indicated, all Scripture quotations are taken from the *King James Version* of the Bible.

Scripture verses marked *TLB* are taken from *The Living Bible*. Copyright © 1971 owned by assignment by Illinois Regional Bank N.A. (as trustee). Used by permission of Tyndale House Publishers, Inc., Wheaton, Illinois 60189. All rights reserved.

30, 60, Hundredfold—
Your Financial Harvest Released

ISBN 0-89274-596-7

Copyright © 1989 by Dr. John Avanzini
Box 1057
Hurst, Texas 76053

Published by Harrison House, Inc.
P.O. Box 35035
Tulsa, Oklahoma 74153

Contents

Preface

Please prepare your heart for a very special time with me in this study. In it I will help you learn and put into practice God's simple laws of the harvest. Our textbook will be the Holy Bible. Our senior teacher will be the Holy Spirit of God. Our purpose will be that your finances will increase so the Gospel can be preached, your needs will be abundantly met, and you will have plenty left over to give joyfully to others. When God asks you to give to Him, you can say, "Yes!"

JOHN AVANZINI

*This book is lovingly dedicated
to my second daughter,
Sherri Lynn,
a twice-given gift of God
to my wife and me.*

1
The Laws of the Harvest

I.   Your seed must be planted!

> ... Except a corn of wheat *fall into the ground* ... it abideth alone ....
> **John 12:24**

II.   You must render your seed useless!

> ... Except a corn of wheat fall into the ground and *die*, it abideth alone ....
> **John 12:24**

III.   You must plant what you expect to harvest!

> ... herb yielding seed *after his kind* ....
> **Genesis 1:12**

IV.   Your harvest size is established when your seed is sown!

> ... A farmer who plants just a few seeds *will get only a small crop*, but if he plants much, *he will reap much.*
> **II Corinthians 9:6 TLB**

V.   Your seed must be planted in good ground!

> ... other (seed) fell into good ground, and brought forth fruit, some an *hundredfold*, some *sixtyfold*, some *thirtyfold.*
> **Matthew 13:8**

VI.   You always wait a period of time between planting and harvesting!

> ... a man should cast seed into the ground;
> And should *sleep*, and *rise night and day*, and the
> seed should spring and grow up . . . .
> **Mark 4:26, 27**

VII.   You must maintain your crops for a proper harvest!

> ... and the *thorns* sprung up, and choked
> them.
> **Matthew 13:7**

VIII.   You always sow to your harvest size, not from your harvest size!

> ... Isaac *sowed* in that land, and *received*
> ... an hundredfold . . . .
> **Genesis 26:12**

IX.   Your expense is always highest at harvest time!

> ... a man that is an householder ... went
> out early in the morning to *hire laborers* into his
> vineyard.
> **Matthew 20:1**

X.   A part of your harvest is for sowing again!

> For God, who gives seed to the farmer *to*
> *plant*, and later on good crops to harvest and eat, will
> give you more and more *seed to plant* . . . .
> **II Corinthians 9:10 TLB**

XI.   A part of your harvest is for you to keep!

> ... who planteth a vineyard, and *eatheth*
> not of *the fruit* thereof?
>
> **I Corinthians 9:7**

XII.   Your harvest is a miracle!

> I have planted, Apollos watered; but
> *God gave the increase.*
>
> **I Corinthians 3:6**

All Truth Is Parallel

God multiplies your money in the same way He multiplies the farmer's seed.   The hundredfold, sixtyfold, or thirtyfold increase is not limited to the agricultural harvest. The tremendous multiplication principle of the harvest pertains to the Christian's money in the same way it pertains to the farmer's seed. These are not the words of a man; they are the words of God.

The Apostle Paul clearly makes this parallel in the book of II Corinthians.

> ... remember this — if you give little, you
> will get little. A farmer who plants just a few seeds
> will get only a small crop, but if he plants much, he
> will reap much.
>
> **II Corinthians 9:6** *TLB*

With this statement, Paul points out that the amount of seed planted directly affects the size of the harvest that will be produced. No one questions that this works on the farm. However, in reading further, it becomes evident that Paul's primary purpose is not to teach the Corinthians how to multiply their agricultural seed. His purpose is to teach them how to multiply their money seed. He is showing them that the same thing that happens when the farmer plants his seed happens when they give their money. *They will experience a harvest!* By this we know there is a parallel between giving money into the Gospel and planting seed into the ground.

Giving Brings Forth Multiplication

> **God is able to make it up to you by giving you everything you need and more, so that there will not only be enough for your own needs, but plenty left over to give joyfully to others.**
> **II Corinthians 9:8 *TLB***

The traditional church teaches it is wrong to give finances to God expecting to receive finances back from God. Even the most uninformed reader of the above Scripture will have to conclude that the traditional church has misunderstood God's Word on this subject.

Notice this verse is not teaching that if you give a certain amount of money, you will receive back the same amount you gave. It speaks of giving an amount of money and then *receiving back more money* than was originally given. It says you will receive *everything you need and much more.*

> **Give, and it shall be given unto you . . . .**
> **Luke 6:38**

There will not be just one single seed of money harvested for each seed of money planted. Multiplied money seeds will be harvested for each money seed that is sown.

> ... it shall be given unto you; good measure, pressed down, and shaken together, and running over ... .
>
> **Luke 6:38**

If you sow a hundred dollars into the Gospel, you will reap many hundreds of dollars back in a money harvest. There is no question about it; God offers the most liberal of terms. Some of His accounts pay a hundredfold increase, others pay a sixtyfold increase, and yet others pay a thirtyfold increase.

> ... (seeds) fell into good ground, and brought forth ... some an hundredfold, some sixtyfold, some thirtyfold.
>
> **Matthew 13:8**

It Is God's Responsibility To Make Up What You Give!

If something is to be made up to you, it stands to reason it is owed to you. Pay attention to this next statement, for a great truth is about to be revealed. When you give your finances to God, *He personally takes the responsibility of making them up to you!*

> **God is able to make it up to you ... .**
> **II Corinthians 9:8 *TLB***

That fact in itself is wonderful, but there is more. God always replaces the amount you have given, *plus* a liberal increase! He not only gives you back enough to meet your own need, but abundantly more than you need.

The greatest benefit of giving to God is that each time you give, you reposition yourself for another harvest. There is no limit to the number of times you are allowed to repeat this process. With each planting of seed, you are promised *everything you need and more so that* (the reason for the surplus) *"there will not only be enough for your own needs, but plenty left over"* (not to hoard and stack up, but) *"to give joyfully to others"* (II Cor. 9:8 *TLB*).

With each cycle of this process, the three-fold purpose of the financial harvest is accomplished.
1. The Gospel is preached.
2. Your needs are abundantly met.
3. You have plenty left over to give joyfully to others.

Your Good Name Is Eternally Established

It is as the Scriptures say: "The godly man gives generously ... His good deeds will be an honor to him forever."

II Corinthians 9:9 *TLB*

According to this verse, your giving establishes you as a good man or woman. If you sow your finances properly, it will bring you honor forever.

Many men and women have awards and plaques adorning their walls. These honors are the good words of man about man. I appreciate the importance of these mementos. The Word of God encourages us to have a good report among men.

However, it is much more valuable to have the Scriptures give us honor. Your understanding of the contents of this book will instruct you in qualifying for this honor. Your proper performance of the laws of the harvest will bring it to pass.

You Have Something To Give

> . . . God who gives seed to the farmer to plant, and later on good crops to harvest and eat, *will give you more and more seed to plant* and will make it grow so that you can give away more and more fruit from your harvest.
> *Yes, God will give you much so that you can give away much . . . .*
>
> **II Corinthians 9:10, 11TLB**

In almost every church in which I speak, in the seminars I conduct, in letters I receive, I hear the same statement again and again: *"Brother John, God has not provided me with any money to give."*

Please believe me. I do not want to incur anyone's wrath. However, I must be faithful to the Word of God. I am duty bound to challenge this scandalous accusation against our God. *Every Christian has money provided to him for the purpose of giving to God.* Look at the Word of God again.

> . . . God who gives seed to the farmer to plant. . .*will give you more and more seed to plant . . . .*
>
> **II Corinthians 9:10 TLB**

I am aware that when the offering plate comes around, there are many Christians who do not have any money to put in it. Please understand, this lack of money does not occur because God did not provide these folks with money to give. The real reason this happens is that they have misappropriated the money God provided for giving. To put it plainly, they have used their seed (money) for something else. They have spent it on themselves or on someone other than God.

There Is a Remedy

The next time you don't have anything to put in the offering plate, try this. Instead of saying, "God did not give me any money, " try saying, "I have *misappropriated* the seed money God gave me to give. Because of this, I do not have any money to put in the offering."

After confessing this, ask God to forgive you; then ask Him to give you an opportunity to make up to Him what you have misused. If you will do this from a sincere heart, God will surely let you make it up to Him. Remember, He is open to this kind of an agreement, for He promises to make up what you give to Him.

> **God is able to make it up to you . . . .**
> **II Corinthians 9:8 *TLB***

Write on your offering envelope that you are going to make up the misused funds. Then, as you make up these misused funds, be careful not to misappropriate your seed again.

This remedy may seem embarrassing, but it is totally effective. Try it. You may not like it, but I guarantee you it will work!

Throughout Christian circles we are constantly confronted with the subject of planting seed. This book is not written to present the seed-faith principle as a new concept. It is written to bring added illumination to the operation of this truth. Each chapter will help establish the proper operation of the seed-faith principle in your life.

Seed Faith Is Not New

Seed-faith giving is not only a New Testament doctrine. It finds its roots in the book of Genesis, where every significant Bible teaching finds its beginning.

Seed faith (faith that a seed will multiply) is the system God depends on to assure the propagation of every life form He created on Earth. Everyone knows plant life continues to exist by the seed-faith principle. Likewise, all animal life is propagated by the seed-faith principle. Even human beings reproduce and multiply according to this same principle.

The first recorded promise of a savior was made to Adam and Eve by the seed-faith principle in the book of Genesis.

> **. . . I will put enmity between thee and the woman, and between thy *seed* and her *seed*; it shall bruise thy head, and thou shalt bruise his heel.**
> **Genesis 3:15**

This first promise of Jesus, the Messiah, was made by God in the form of a seed-faith promise. It would be the seed of the woman who would deliver mankind from the curse.

The Church Exists Today
Through the Seed-Faith Principle!

> ... I will make of thee a great nation, and I will bless thee, and make thy name great; and thou shalt be a blessing:
> And I will bless them that bless thee, and curse him that curseth thee: and in thee shall all families of the earth be blessed.
> Genesis 12:2, 3

> ... if ye be Christ's, then are ye Abraham's seed, and heirs according to the promise.
> Galatians 3:29

From this early promise made to Abram came the glorious Church with its ultimate commission to bless all the families of the earth. The promise of the Church has existed through thousands of years by way of the seed-faith principle.

Planting financial seed is the God-ordained way to multiply your money. With this said, I can hear someone saying, *"Brother John, that is not the way my ultra-modern, hi-tech bank multiplies money. That seed-faith business is old-fashioned and out of date."*

Rather than arguing about this, just read the newspapers. Banks — I mean ultra-modern, hi-tech banks — fail almost daily. Keep in mind that this modern banking system has brought the nations of the world to the brink of economic collapse.

God's Harvest Principle
Is a Higher Principle

Before you dismiss God's method as being impractical, please realize He does not think like we do.

> **. . . My thoughts are not your thoughts, neither are your ways my ways, saith the Lord. For as the heavens are higher than the earth, so are my ways higher than your ways, and my thoughts than your thoughts.**
> **Isaiah 55:8, 9**

If you are so foolish as to consider man's monetary system superior to God's, just remember God's system has *never* failed. Man's systems fail daily. God's ways are superior, for they come to us from His ultimately superior mind. Seeding to a financial harvest is totally God's idea, not man's. He is the only One who promises that when you give to Him, He will give back to you — some a hundredfold, some sixtyfold, and some thirtyfold.

The farmer cannot multiply his seed by the use of inside information or manipulation. If a harvest is to be experienced, God must perform the miracle of increase inside each seed. God alone is able to multiply your seed into a harvest.

Understanding Farming
Is Important to Your Financial Harvest

It is important for believers to have a basic understanding of farming. When I first came into the Bible revelation of multiplying money, I knew almost nothing about farming. I had grown up in the city. My lack of farm knowledge was a continual hindrance to me. I found it very difficult to bring forth a successful financial harvest without some basic farming knowledge.

Many of you readers are faced with this same problem. You live in the age of astronauts, computer whizzes, and advanced technology; yet the Holy Bible is a book that was originally written in the language of farmers, using illustrations common to farmers. With this book, we must discern God's will for our lives.

Do not misunderstand. Your Bible is not obsolete. It can still answer your every need. People in the hi-tech age still eat food that comes from the farm. They continue to be born in the same way the first farmer, Cain, was born. They still face the same basic problems and challenges that past cultures and civilizations have faced.

Your Bible contains the answers to all your needs in every realm. It matters not whether it be salvation, child-rearing, or basic living. There is a parallel between the problems of the farmer in ancient Israel, the pioneer on the early frontier, and the astronaut in space. The dilemma is not that the Word of God does not contain the answers to life's most important questions. The problem is that many of us do not have command of enough farm knowledge to fully understand what it says.

God's Principles Do Not Change

Just because we do not fully understand God's laws of the

harvest does not mean they are not still in operation. Not one of God's laws is dependent upon your understanding of it for it to work. God's laws operate, not because of your knowledge of them, but in *spite* of your knowledge of them.

Just because I do not fully understand the law of gravity does not mean it will not operate on my body. I won't just float off the planet because I don't happen to know all there is to know about it. If I step off the top floor of the Empire State Building, my ignorance of God's law of gravity will not excuse me from its consequences.

The laws of the harvest operate whether you understand them or not. If you understand and obey them, they will bless you with a harvest. If you are ignorant of them, they will operate against you, leaving you in shortage instead of abundance.

The Truth Will Set You Free?

The following verse of Scripture is one of the most important verses in the Bible. In spite of its importance, it remains almost universally misunderstood.

> **. . . ye shall know the truth, and the truth shall make you free.**
> **John 8:32**

This verse does not say what most Christians think it says. It does not say the truth will set you free. It says *the truth you know* will set you free. You cannot enjoy the freedom that any truth in God's Word promises unless you know about it.

Every Christian who wants to be set free in finances must know the truth of God's financial principles.

When I realized how ignorant I was about basic farming principles, I made up my mind to learn something about them. As I did, I learned God's laws of the financial harvest are the same as His laws of the agricultural harvest. I gained this knowledge primarily in two ways — by studying the Word of God and by discussing what I learned from it with farmers. This combination gave me the valuable insight I needed to greatly increase my finances.

Ironically, every farmer with whom I discussed the parallel between farming and finances asked for a copy of this book. That made me realize I was not just writing a book for the city dweller, but I was writing a book for Christians everywhere. We all need to know how to operate the laws of the harvest so God can multiply our finances.

2

The First Law of the Harvest:
Your Seed Must Be Planted

(There is) **a time to** *plant,* **and a time to pluck
up that which is** *planted.*
Ecclesiastes 3:2

Solomon does not say there is only a time for plucking
up, but he says there is a time for plucking up *that which has
been planted.*

The writer of Genesis quotes God as saying,

**While the earth remaineth, seedtime and
harvest . . . shall not cease.**
Genesis 8:22

Once again, it is not just harvest time but *seedtime* and
harvest time. Without *seedtime,* it is impossible to have
harvest time.

Jesus reinforced this truth when He said that if a grain of
wheat doesn't fall into the ground (seedtime), it abides alone
(never multiplies into a harvest).

**Verily, verily, I say unto you, Except a corn
of wheat** *fall into the ground* **. . . it abideth
alone . . . .**
John 12:24

This is a truth you must understand if you expect to
receive money from God. Many well-meaning Christians

live their entire lives without ever learning that giving money is essential to reaping a money harvest. No matter how fertile the ground, no matter how strong the seed, if that seed does not get planted, it cannot multiply. It will abide alone.

Unplanted Seeds Do Have Benefits

There are many uses for seeds other than planting them. They vary from food to costume jewelry. Seed can be ground into meal, and from that meal, delicious hot breads, desserts, and even dressings, can be made. These delicacies can stimulate the taste buds of the most discriminating eater. Cattle and livestock can be fed with seeds, bringing forth healthy, full-grown animals. Even the wild game of the fields enjoy a benefit from seeds.

But not one seed that is eaten or fed to a cow will ever multiply itself into hundreds of other seeds. It must follow the procedure ordained by Jesus. That is, it must fall into the earth. Your seed must be planted before it will multiply.

Seed Necklaces Do Not Multiply

I am reminded of a very special vacation my wife and I took over fifteen years ago. The church we were pastoring at the time graciously sent us to the beautiful Hawaiian Islands for a much needed rest.

As was our custom on this type of journey, we looked for a suitable souvenir to bring back to our church members. Our congregation was over one-thousand members strong at that time, so we needed a nice gift, priced to fit our budget. We found just the right thing — beautiful, handmade, necklaces made of various tropical seeds. As you can imagine, there was a great stir at the church on our return and subsequent gift giving.

Much to our surprise and delight, we met one of our former members from that church a few months ago. We were so very glad to see her and renew our acquaintance with this dear saint. As we spoke, she said she had something special to show us. Well, you can imagine our surprise when she brought forth the necklace that we had given her those many years ago. It was still in like-new condition, shiny and bright. I couldn't help but notice that even though almost fifteen years had passed, not one of the seeds on her necklace had multiplied. They were exactly as they had been on the day we gave them to her. Why? Because Jesus, the creator of seed, said if the seed doesn't fall into the ground, it cannot multiply. It will abide alone.

Seed can fall into the hands of the artist, and with it he can make beautiful jewelry. However, polishing and crafting a seed cannot multiply it. Seed can fall into the kettle of some fine cook, and it can bring forth a meal fit for a king, but cooking a seed cannot multiply it. There is only one way to multiply a seed. It has to be planted. This is a law of the harvest that cannot be altered.

The first law of the financial harvest is parallel with the first law of the agricultural harvest. God cannot bring forth a financial harvest for you unless you plant a part of your finances into the Gospel.

It's Not Working, Brother John!

I am continuously confronted by Christians who have financial needs. They come to me complaining that their giving hasn't produced a harvest. When they speak to me of the hard times and failures they are experiencing, it appears as if they want me to say, "You do not have to give anymore."

Dear friend, I do not have the authority to do that. It is true that I have an anointing, and I do have a ministry that is seen daily across America on television; but even with the few seemingly impressive things that can be said about me, I do not have the authority to change God's laws of the harvest. God has said, unless your financial seed falls into the ground (gets planted in the Gospel), it abides alone.

If you are sowing but not reaping, the problem is not with God's laws of the harvest. It has to be something else, for the laws of the harvest work.

Usually when I question these people who are having trouble harvesting finances, I find they have failed to tell me some very important things about their Christian lives. Maybe they have just started giving, not allowing time for the harvest to grow. Maybe they don't tithe regularly, thus blocking their harvest because the windows of heaven cannot be opened to them. For one reason or another, they are not properly getting their financial seed into the good ground of the Gospel.

It doesn't matter how sincere you may be. It doesn't matter how great your need is. It doesn't matter how religious you are. If you want to experience a harvest in your finances, you must comply with God's laws of the harvest. This is the first law: There cannot be a harvest until a seed has been planted. God cannot increase finances until some finances have been given to Him.

The Most Popular Verse About Giving and Receiving

The most popular New Testament verse of Scripture dealing with receiving begins with this simple condition-- something must first be given.

> **Give, and it shall be given unto you; good measure, pressed down, and shaken together, and running over, shall men give into your bosom. For with the same measure that ye mete withal it shall be measured to you again.**
>
> **Luke 6:38**

Notice the word "give" (or sow). There cannot be full baskets of grain, running over, pressed down, until some grain has been given. Neither can there be full baskets of money pressed down and running over until some money has been given into the Gospel.

Scripture abounds with this premise of seeding to a harvest. When Solomon tells us bread will come to us on the water, he predicates this on a specific action. He says we must give (sow) some bread on the water first.

> *Cast thy bread upon the waters;* **for thou shalt find it after many days.**
>
> **Ecclesiastes 11:1**

How nice it would be if there were an eternal incoming tide of bread. Why, all we would have to do is daily gather up the staff of life, living the good life without ever having to sow. As nice as this would be, it just will not happen that way. God says a seed must fall into the ground, or it abides alone. The truth is, the appearance of bread in our lives depends upon the distribution of bread into the lives of others.

Every aspect of increase operates in parallel with this principle. For instance, if you want people to be friendly, first plant a seed of friendliness.

Even the universally respected golden rule operates on this premise.

> **... all things whatsoever ye would that men**
> **should do to you, do ye even so to them . . . .**
> **Matthew 7:12**

Whatever you wish to receive from others, you must first plant into their lives. There must be a seed planted before a harvest can be reaped.

Planted Seeds Always Bring Forth Fruit

My wife and I have planted seeds of service, seeds of love, seeds of loyalty, and seeds of finance many times. Each time we have sown these seeds, they have come up multiplied in our lives.

In the realm of service, we sowed into the lives of many elderly and sick folks in our past years of ministry. There were so many, we cannot even remember them all. Now, many years later, we have a great harvest of service going on in our lives. Everywhere we go, doors are opened for us and our baggage is carried. As we travel, we are literally waited on hand and foot. I must admit that sometimes it is embarrassing how folks fuss over us. I now realize we created this atmosphere by sowing this atmosphere into the lives of others.

This same thing has happened from the seeds of love we have sown in the lives of church members, ministers, and missionaries. In times past people from all over the world have stayed in our home, driven our cars, found open arms and loving, sympathetic hearts. The two primary churches we pastored were always identified, above everything else, as churches full of love.

Now, as Pat and I travel worldwide, we find such fervent love everywhere we go that it overwhelms us. From Alaska to South America, from the Caribbean to the Hawaiian Islands, from Asia to Africa, letters and tokens of love come to us almost daily.

We are reaping a great harvest of love and loyalty from seeds we have sown in the past. In almost every city in America, and in many nations of the world, pastors and laymen stand with our ministry. They recommend us to others and encourage us to come back again and again. Loyal, loving brothers and sisters are on every hand.

My wife and I are constantly speaking to each other of the wonderful lives that God allows us to live. I do not want to take away from the power and the goodness of God by what I am saying. However, I am convinced that if Pat and I had not sown the seeds of service, love, and loyalty, our present lives would be very different.

It would have been easier for us not to have sown the seeds of service. We could have just been polite and not gotten involved in the lives of others. How easy it would have been simply to isolate ourselves from others. But God's Word warned us that without love, we would be nothing. Our lives would be as the unplanted seed. We would abide alone!

How glad I am for every seed of love and service we ever planted! For now, in our fifties, when many husbands and wives begin what are called the "lonely years," Pat and I begin the most active part of our lives with a rich harvest of love from both new and old friends. Thank God that our seed was planted to harvest.

An Investment Must Be Made
To Draw Increase

This same sowing and reaping process has also brought us a bountiful financial harvest. Throughout our lives we have sown our finances liberally.

I cannot help but remember, as young Christians at Bible college in Springfield, Missouri, Pastor Fred Needy of Southside Baptist Church taught us to give beyond our tithe to world missions. We began with $3.00 per week. Our total weekly income then was barely $40.00. How hard it was, but faithfully, each week, we gave our $4.00 tithe and $3.00 mission offering.

In time, both our tithe and our mission offering grew substantially. We sowed for years, and today the harvest is evident as our ministry receives funds daily from around the world. This would never have happened if we had not been taught to plant our seed in the good ground of the Gospel.

There came a time when our church was in a position to purchase a new car for us. I remember what we did with that new car. We gave it to a missionary to drive. It was brand new, right out of the showroom. He kept it for a full year before it was brought back to us. It then had 80,000 miles on it, but instead of driving it, we sent it with another missionary for another year. My wife inherited it with well over 100,000 miles. She then drove it for another two years before it was given away again.

Again the church bought a new car for us, and instead of driving it, another missionary drove it for a year and a half, returning it with over 90,000 miles. I drove it after that for two more years before it was given away again.

Many people might say, "How foolish! Why not drive the new car first yourself. Then let the missionary drive it when it is old?"

Dear friend, wake up! If we had sown old cars, we would now be reaping old cars. We knew the laws of the harvest, so we sowed new cars. Now my wife and I both drive new cars. If we chose to, we could drive a new one every year. But, we couldn't reap a harvest of cars until we had been faithful in planting cars, for a seed must be planted, or it abides alone.

Financial Institutions
Follow This Same Law

Without making an investment, not one financial institution will give you an increase. Every commercial bank account bears interest only on the amount of money invested into that account. No matter how high the interest rate at a lending institution may be, that institution will pay no increase unless there has been a deposit made.

The financial increase from your bank is much different than the harvest that comes from God. Compared to God, the world's banking system is very stingy in its rate of increase. Most bank saving plans barely creep above 4% interest per year. Their more generous accounts allow a meager 6% to 8%. They have such restrictions as minimum deposits, lengthy time of deposit, and substantial penalties for any deviation.

Do not think God is a fool just because He is generous. He still demands that a deposit be made before an increase can be realized.

Be not deceived; God is not mocked: for
whatsoever a man soweth, that shall he also reap.
Galatians 6:7

Just as the increase of the agricultural harvest demands that a seed must be planted, so the increase of your finances demands that some of your finances must be planted.

Allow this first universal law of the harvest to sink deep

into your spirit, and let it become a basic premise in your life. As you do, you will find its benefit will keep you in abundance in your later years.

Law #1: Your seed must be planted.

3

The Second Law of the Harvest:
You Must Render Your Seed Useless

Except a corn of wheat fall into the ground and
die, it abideth alone . . . .

John 12:24

The people of God often give in such a way that their seed gives them some personal benefit. King David was once faced with an opportunity to do this. He went to a certain place to make a very special sacrifice to God. II Samuel 24:18-25 tells the story of this event.

Because the place was far from his home, it was necessary for him to buy the sacrificial animals from a local landowner. The owner of the property very graciously offered to supply King David with all the animals for the sacrifice completely free of charge.

Now this was a very kind gesture on the part of the landowner; however, David quickly rejected it. He wisely refused to sacrifice to His God that which had cost him nothing. Hear the scriptural account as he boldly answered the man who so generously tried to bless him.

. . . neither will I offer burnt offerings unto
the Lord my God of that which doth cost me
nothing . . . .

II Samuel 24:24

David knew that an offering which cost him nothing would bring him absolutely no benefit from God. The offering had to cost David something so he could show God his love for Him.

Throughout the church I am constantly meeting people who seem to be ignorant of this biblical principle. They are giving if it does not cost them anything. They are giving with some secondary benefit to themselves. This cannot bring a financial harvest. Before I list some of these ineffective forms of giving, look again at the words of Jesus on this matter. They clearly teach that our seed gift must become of no use to us before He can multiply it back to us.

Verily, verily I say unto you, except a corn of wheat fall into the ground *and die*, it abideth alone: but if it die, *it bringeth forth much fruit.*
John 12:24

When our Lord said the seed must die before it can accomplish the miracle of multiplication, he meant it must enter a stage of uselessness to the planter. When a planted seed enters the stage of death, the farmer can no longer eat it. He cannot sell it. He cannot feed it to his livestock. For all intents and purposes it has become totally useless to him; it has died.

This same thing must happen to our financial seed when it is sown into the work of the Lord. It must leave our control and cease to benefit us. It must be given totally into the hands and control of those who preach the Gospel.

There Is a Kind of Giving
That Brings No Harvest

Let me be quick to say that I am not making the following statements to hurt or bring condemnation to anyone. I am making them to bring illumination. I am believing that by illumination, conviction will come. Then conviction will lead the violators into a more effective and productive form of giving.

Consider the person who is helping one or more of his children through some difficult financial times. Maybe it is a daughter who has suffered the misfortune of a divorce. Many times in this unfortunate circumstance, there are minor children she is responsible for supporting.

In a situation like this I often hear parents say they are giving a part of their tithes and offerings to help their daughter and her children. These well-meaning folks almost always add that they are sure God approves. They may even quote 1 Timothy 5:8 to me, saying,

> ... if any provide not for his own, and specially
> for those of his own house, he hath denied the faith,
> and is worse than an infidel.

Now, do not misunderstand. There is nothing wrong with caring for your own. In fact, according to the Scripture just quoted, it is not optional. This and other verses clearly teach us that it is our responsibility to do so. However, using our tithes and offerings to do this is not based on any teaching I have found in the Word of God. In the Bible we are given explicit instructions as to where the tithe is to be given.

**Bring ye *all* the tithes into the storehouse,
that there may be meat in mine house . . . .
Malachi 3:10**

It does not say to bring a portion of your tithe to your daughter's house that there may be food in her house. Instead, it clearly says to bring *all* the tithe into God's house that there may be meat in *His* house.

Yes, we are to provide for our own. But we are to do so *after the tithe (10%) and the offering (an optional amount) have been given to God.*

If we use the tithe and the offering to meet our personal obligations, we are not letting that seed die. We are not letting it become useless to us. If your seed is to be multiplied, it must, as our Lord said, fall into the ground *and die*, or it will abide alone. It cannot multiply unless it becomes useless to you.

Let me emphasize again, I am not telling anyone not to help their children in their hour of need. However, I am saying do not to use the money God has designated for His purposes to accomplish your own purposes. Give God that which is His and trust Him to supply you with the extra finances needed to meet the additional expenses you face.

My Wife and I Overcame This Problem

My wife and I faced the crisis of divorce with both of our precious daughters at the same time. Try as we might, there was no averting this tragedy, as both of our daughters' marriages ended.

38

This happened just as we thought we were about to have some time to ourselves. We had just seen our youngest of five children married. Then, without notice, we were confronted with both daughters and their five children, without husbands and without adequate means of support. While both daughters did have jobs, a good portion of their support became our responsibility.

Now, I must be honest. This all happened at a most inconvenient time for us financially. It would have been very easy for us to dip into the tithe and redirect it from the house of God into the hands of our two daughters. Knowing my girls, I am sure they would have used it ever so carefully and only for the best of purposes. What a financial relief it would have been to us if we would have done this.

But we could not do it because the Scriptures clearly say that *all* the tithe is the Lord's. It is holy unto Him.

> **. . . *all* the tithe of the land, whether of the seed of the land, or of the fruit of the tree, is the Lord's: it is holy unto the Lord.**
> **Leviticus 27:30**

We had no options when it came to the Lord's money, so we continued to give our tithe and generous offerings into the house of God. We understood we had to strictly obey the second law of the harvest. The seed we planted had to die (become of no use to us).

If we would have used the Lord's tithes and offering money to supplement our daughters' living, no doubt it would have been a blessing to them. However, the money we would have given them would never have been multiplied back to us.

Before a seed can grow into a harvest, it must become useless to the sower. Or, as Jesus said,

> ... Except a corn of wheat fall into the ground
> and die, it abides alone . . . .
> **John 12:24**

As my wife and I reached out to help our daughters, we were being financially stretched to our limits. Fortunately, we knew God's plan for the multiplication of money sown into His Gospel. Because of this, we began giving special offerings (planting extra seed), reaching out to God for an even greater harvest to help us with our new responsibilities. We stayed faithful in tithing and increased our offerings whenever possible.

God proved Himself and His Word to be faithful by reaching back to us and actually increasing our income. I am happy to report that God did what He promised in II Corinthians 9:8-9. *He made it up to us* by giving us everything we needed and more, so that there was not only enough for our own needs, but plenty left over to give joyfully toward the needs of our daughters and their five children.

Because of God's unfailing harvest plan, we never once had to feel bitter over the added expense. As the Scripture said, we truly could give joyfully to our daughters.

Tithes and Offerings
Are Not for Educating Your Children

Another common misuse people make of their tithe and offering money is to educate their children. I am often confronted by well-meaning people who tell me they are tithers, and they give offerings, but for some strange reason they are not seeing a harvest from their seed. Upon closer examination it is revealed that because of a special tuition benefit, they are presently sending their tithe money to the Bible college their child attends.

This type of so-called "giving" is not letting your seed fall into the ground and die. This is making God pay for your child's education. Whenever your tithe is diverted to educate your child, it cannot be multiplied back to you in a harvest.

Now, I realize every one of those dollars will be a benefit to you and your child, but not one of them will ever multiply into a harvest. For Jesus, the Lord, the One who rules over the harvest, says that if a seed does not fall into the good ground and die (become of no value to you), it abides alone.

I do not want to stir up any confusion in church-owned schools, but using the memberships' tithe as tuition is a very dangerous practice, for it renders the seed impotent and incapable of multiplication. I suggest that if you are involved in any such practice, you immediately meet with your pastor and discuss the scriptural aspects of this arrangement.

"Oh, Pastor, You Can Have It All When I Die!"

Another common practice that spoils the harvest is when a person holds back all assets from God until death. I know people who do not tithe or give offerings, believing they are entitled to all of the benefits of a bountiful harvest.

These mistaken folks base that notion on the fact that, at their death, they have designated a large sum of money to be left to gospel outreaches. These folks rationalize that since they will be leaving the ministry a large amount of money at death, surely God is pleased. However, this is not their only motivation. They think this is a smart way to enjoy what they have while they are alive. Please notice some interesting things about this kind of *giving evasion*.

First of all, the person who releases his tithes and offerings into the ministry at his death does not give anything to the Lord. He simply *leaves* everything. I am not saying we should not leave something substantial to the work of God when we die. This is a wonderful thing to do and can be of immeasurable benefit to the Gospel, however this is not planting a seed. It is not a form of giving. It is a form of controlled leaving.

There is a second reason why this is not a proper way to pay tithes or plant seed. Seed that is planted must bring forth a harvest. However, everyone knows there will not be any use for money in heaven. The saint of God who defers giving his tithes and offerings, leaving them at his death, cannot receive a harvest from them. He is no longer in the land of the living, where harvests can occur.

When Jesus spoke to the rich young ruler He said,

> ... There is no man that hath left house ... or lands, for my sake, and the gospel's, But he shall receive an hundredfold *now in this time*, houses ... and lands ... .
>
> **Mark 10:29, 30**

Harvest takes place *now, in this time*. Harvest is unique to the land of the living. You do not harvest money, houses, or lands after death. Holding the tithe until death is not a biblical way of giving.

Do It According to the Book

If it is your desire to reap a financial harvest, you are going to have to obey God's simple laws of the harvest. Your seed will have to be planted without any secondary benefits to you. It will have to fall into the ground and die. Remember the two laws we have studied.

Law #1: Your seed must be planted.
Law #2: You must render your seed useless.

4

The Third Law of the Harvest:
You Must Plant
What You Expect To Harvest

> . . . the earth brought forth grass, and herb
> yielding seed *after his kind* . . . .
> **Genesis 1:12**

It has been wisely said that the biggest fool in town is the one who fools himself. Believe it or not, people do fool themselves. It happens all the time. God warns us of the potential of this folly in the realm of sowing and reaping.

> *Be not deceived;* God is not mocked: for *what-soever* a man soweth, *that* shall he also reap.
> **Galatians 6:7**

It is amazing that God would have to warn His people of such an obvious error! Yet He felt it necessary to tell those who sow not to fool themselves. This is such a simple truth that it seems as if it should not even have to be said.

Everyone knows apple seeds will always bring forth a harvest of apples, and peach seeds will always bring forth a harvest of peaches. Every seed always produces a harvest *after its own kind*. It has always been that way. It is that way today.

This agricultural information was well-known to the people to whom Paul wrote in his epistle. Nevertheless, precious space is taken in the Holy Writ to warn the reader. From this we must assume there is a potential to make this mistake.

You Cannot Fool God

Not only does Paul warn us not to deceive ourselves, but he emphasizes that we should not attempt to fool God! Hear his words: **Be not deceived; God is not mocked** (made a fool of or deceived). You cannot fool the God of the harvest, for He is the one who established the foolproof laws of the harvest. They are unchanging.

This law is set in time and in eternity. It is irreversible. The kind of seed you sow always determines the kind of harvest you will reap. By some ingenious method, you may disguise an apple seed to look like a peach seed. But when it grows to full stature, it will bring forth an apple tree that bears apples, not peaches.

If you put a hundred-dollar bill in an envelope and mail it to your favorite television ministry, the one hundred dollars is the seed, not the envelope that conceals it. God will not be fooled and send you a harvest of envelopes. He will send you a harvest of hundred-dollar bills.

They Say Giving to God Doesn't Work

Every so often I hear uninformed people say that giving to God doesn't work. Many of them are very good people who really love God. Their problem is not a lack of sincerity but a lack of knowledge. They are ignorant of some, or all, of His laws of the harvest. God says if a seed is planted and germinates, it will bring forth *in kind*. To think otherwise is to make a fool of yourself.

There are various reasons why people are not satisfied with the harvest their seed brings forth. Some even feel that after they have sown, there has been no harvest at all. Please remember — it is not the kind of harvest you need that determines the kind of harvest you will receive. It is the *kind of seed you plant* that determines the kind of harvest you will reap.

Let me give you an illustration from my own experience. Some years ago, a precious person came to me in a very respectful manner. He asked me to help him understand why the principle of seed giving had not worked in his dear mother's life. This person related to me in much detail how precious his mother was and of her unswerving devotion to God. She had visited the sick. She had cooked delicious meals for shut-ins.

She had also made many beautiful afghans for her friends and relatives. These afghans were painstakingly handwoven and delivered to twenty-five or more people over the course of the dear woman's active years. However, now in her last years, no great financial harvest had been manifested because of her giving. Actually, just the opposite had occurred. She was now penniless and had to be cared for in a welfare nursing home.

Then came the painful part. With tears in his eyes, this precious son asked, "Why wasn't my mother's generous giving honored by God? She gave unselfishly, but now she is on welfare like a common pauper."

I must say, I was careful in my answer to this dear person, for he was convinced that Jehovah God had not kept His promise to his dear mother.

> **Give, and it shall be given unto you . . . .**
> **Luke 6:38**

Many times when folks approach me to question God's Word, they are less than sincere. This man, however, was refreshingly different. I believed every word he had spoken of his dear mother's godly, caring life. I believed him when he said his mother had been a consistent giver. I believed him when he told me she was a good woman who loved God and loved her fellow man. When I answered his question, I began with the Word of God.

> **Be not deceived; God is not mocked: for whatsoever a man soweth, that shall he also reap.**
> **Galatians 6:7**

Remember, this dear person's mother had sown *visits to the sick, meals to the shut-ins,* and *afghans to friends and relatives.* I carefully questioned him about his mother's present status.

"Does your mother ever have any *visitors* at the nursing home?"

There was a pause before the answer came. Then he said, "Yes, there is usually a major traffic jam at her door, both during and after visiting hours."

My next question was answered more quickly and with a new look of understanding. I asked, "Do folks ever bring your mother *meals* or desserts to the nursing home?"

"Why, the doctors and nurses have a terrible time keeping her on a proper diet. People smuggle all sorts of goodies to her every day."

The next words out of his mouth were, "I know your next question! Does she ever receive any *afghans?* Yes, Brother John! Her room and her closet are full of afghans! They come to her, not only from local folks, but sometimes afghans even come to her from other countries!"

In closing this story, you will quickly see what this woman's problem was. When I asked this person if his mother had been faithful in giving tithes and offerings, he quickly stated that neither he nor his mother believed in tithing. They believed it was Old Testament and no longer necessary for our day. They also believed that excessive offerings were being taken by today's ministers. They had made it a practice not to give to any ministry that asked for money. Our conversation ended abruptly. His mind was closed on the subject.

It Is a Big Word

Carefully read our Lord's words from Luke 6:38 again: "Give, and *it* shall be given unto you. . ." Notice the word, *it*. *It* represents whatever you have given.

Let me paraphrase. Give apples, and *it* (apples) will be given unto you. Give peaches, and *it* (peaches) will be given unto you. Give afghans, and *it* (afghans) will be given unto you. Give meals, and *it* (meals) will be given unto you.

Now read this very carefully. *Give money, and it* (money) *will be given unto you,* good measure, pressed down and shaken together, and running over, shall men pour money into your bosom. For with the same measure that you give *money, it* (money) *will be given back to you!*

Get it into your spirit. God will not be mocked. You cannot fool Him. Whatever you sow (give) is exactly what you will reap. God never gets things mixed up in the harvest. You cannot sow afghans and reap retirement income.

To reap retirement income, you must plant a part of your present income into the Gospel. Even our mixed-up government retirement system won't give you Social Security benefits unless you have previously sown money into the Social Security system.

A good understanding of this third law of the harvest will keep you in comfort, far from the clutches of poverty and insufficiency all the way through the last days of your life.

Satanic Interference
Obscures the Laws of the Harvest

Notice that satanic interference is intimated when Paul says, "Be not deceived." Deception is one of the devil's primary powers.

> . . . the great dragon was cast out, that old serpent, called the Devil, and Satan, which *deceiveth* the whole world . . . .
> **Revelation 12:9**

This is the same kind of deception that caused the fall of mankind in the Garden of Eden. Adam and Eve were deceived. They thought they could fool God. They made clothes of leaves, and they hid in the garden, supposing God would not notice they were naked. (Gen. 3:7-10.)

Don't let Satan deceive you. Adam and Eve could not fool God then, and you will not be able to fool Him now. God is not mocked. Whatever you sow, *that* is what you will reap!

Putting Galatians 6:6-10 in Its Proper Context

If you take a close look at Galatians 6:6-10, you will find it is set in a financial context:

> **Let him that is taught in the word communicate (give) unto him that teacheth in all good things.**
> **Be not deceived; God is not mocked: for whatsoever a man soweth, that shall he also reap.**
> **For he that soweth to his flesh shall of the flesh reap corruption; but he that soweth to the Spirit shall of the Spirit reap life everlasting.**
> **And let us not be weary in well doing: for in due season we shall reap, if we faint not.**
> **As we have therefore opportunity, let us do good unto all men, especially unto them who are of the household of faith.**

This passage of Scripture teaches us of God's requirement to give a portion of our finances (good things) to those who teach us the Word of God. It goes on to promise a harvest to those who do not grow weary in well doing (giving to their teachers). It makes a very definite promise that the person who sows finances into the lives of his Bible instructors will reap finances if he doesn't grow impatient while waiting for the harvest.

Notice that the laws of the harvest become clearer each time we learn a new one. They have a logical pattern. When you know and practice all of them, your finances will begin to multiply in the same way the farmer's seed is multiplied.

The three laws we have learned to this point are:

Law #1: Your seed must be planted.
Law #2: You must render your seed useless.
Law #3: You must plant what you expect to harvest.

> **Be not deceived; God is not mocked: for
> whatsoever a man soweth, that shall he also reap.**
> **Galatians 6:7**

Sow tomato seeds, and God's law of the harvest guarantees you will reap tomatoes.

Sow bean seeds, and God's law of the harvest guarantees you will reap beans.

Sow *money* seeds, and God's law of the harvest guarantees you will reap *money*.

No fooling! You have God's Word on it.

5

The Fourth Law of the Harvest:
Your Harvest Size Is Established When Your Seed Is Sown

> ... A farmer who plants just a *few* seeds will get only a *small* crop, but if he plants *much*, he will *reap much*.
>
> **II Corinthians 9:6 *TLB***

In the ninth chapter of the book of II Corinthians, the Apostle Paul makes a distinct parallel between planting seed and giving money to the ministry. In this statement he confirms the fourth law of the harvest.

> ... remember this — if you *give little*, you will *get little*. A farmer who plants just a few seeds will get only a small crop, but if he plants much, he will reap much.
>
> **II Corinthians 9:6 *TLB***

No matter how convenient it would be, you cannot wait until the day of harvest to decide the size of your harvest. If that were possible, the farmer would never face shortage. Just prior to harvest time, he would determine how much harvest he needed, then sow accordingly. If his needs were great, he would plant much. If his needs were small, he would only have to plant a few seeds.

How nice it would be if it were so. Unfortunately, that's not the way the law of the harvest operates. There is always a season (a reasonable period of time) between the time of

53

sowing and the time of harvesting. The farmer must determine the size harvest he will need months before the actual time of harvest arrives. If he plants too little in the spring (sowing time), he will be disappointed in the fall (harvest time).

Abundance Is Preferable to Shortage

I have made an interesting observation during my adult years. It is much easier to adjust to the problem of having more than enough than it is to adjust to the problem of having too little. Shortage always calls for unpleasant actions.

While I was conducting revival services in my early ministry, I began to see evidence of this truth of abundance and shortage. I was preaching in a small community in the heart of the nation's wheat belt. The area had been blessed with successive bumper crops of wheat. That particular year, the harvest was the largest ever recorded. All the grain storage bins across that part of the country were already full. Wheat was everywhere. Even an abandoned school gymnasium was stacked full. Every possible means of storage was filled to capacity. Out of desperation, the grain was being heaped up in the fields on large tarpaulins. I saw that abundance brings with it some real problems and aggravation.

Some years later, I visited rural parts of Africa in a time when crops had failed for several years. There I witnessed just the opposite condition — famine. All the garners were empty. Stomachs were empty. No money came in to pay the farmers' debts. Not a bag of wheat could be found anywhere. Men had to borrow, and even beg. That is when I realized there is no comparison between the gravity of the problems caused by shortage and those caused by abundance.

Wise farmers know they must always plant more than they might need, for it is much easier to adjust to the problem of having more than enough than it is to adjust to the problem of having too little.

Christians Sometimes Miss This Principle

As unbelievable as it may sound, I have heard Christian people say they did not need to give much to God because they did not need much to be happy. By some misguided piety, they reasoned it was spiritual not to desire more than enough.

I am convinced this attitude is nothing more than an attempt to cover up their lack of faith to believe God for more than enough. Ignorance of God's purpose, coupled with insufficient faith in His power to give an increase, brings men to this unscriptural conclusion.

How narrow some Christians' vision has become! How short-sighted we are when we lose the scriptural purpose of abundance. Most Christians I meet are happy to have *only* enough. They would never dare to boldly pray for *more than enough.*

Their conservative position sounds very spiritual. "Oh, God, just give me enough to meet my needs, and I will be satisfied." It is this mentality that has spawned songs like, "Just give me a little cabin in the corner of Glory," and ". . . hardly a comfort can afford."

You Need More Than Enough To Be a Good Christian

Dear Christian friend, you cannot be the Christian God is calling you to be if you have only enough. When you have only enough, you are assured of not having enough to do God's will. When you have only enough, you do not have the ability to fulfill the covenant God made with Abraham. Remember, you are the seed of Abraham.

> **. . . if ye be Christ's, then are ye Abraham's seed, and heirs according to the promise.**
> **Galatians 3:29**

What did God promise the world that you, the seed of Abraham would be?

> **Now the Lord had said unto Abram, Get thee out of thy country, and from thy kindred, and from thy father's house, unto a land that I will shew thee:**
> **And I will make of thee a great nation, and I will bless thee, and make thy name great; and *thou shalt be a blessing*:**
> **And I will bless them that bless thee, and curse him that curseth thee: and *in thee shall all families of the earth be blessed.***
> **Genesis 12:1-3**

As the seed of Abraham, you are to *be a blessing* to all the world. When God says all the families of the earth, He literally means you will be a blessing to every family on planet Earth. This means you have been promised to the lost of this world — promised to *be a blessing to every one of them.*

56

You Cannot Be a Blessing
If You Have Not Been Blessed

It is an impossibility for you to be a blessing to anyone, much less all the families of the earth, unless you have been blessed. I mean you must be blessed beyond that which only meets your own needs. God expects us to fulfill His promise of blessing the world. He told us to feed the hungry and to clothe the naked. (James 2:15-17.)

How can you possibly feed others if you receive only enough to feed yourself? How will you clothe the naked if you receive only enough money to buy your own clothing? The reason God wants you to have more than enough is not to selfishly hide it away. God wants abundance in your life so you can cheerfully meet the needs of others. The Scripture actually says He wants you to have plenty left over after meeting your own needs to give joyfully to others.

> **God is able to make it** (that which you give) **up to you by giving you everything you need and more, so that there will not only be enough for your own needs, but plenty left over to give joyfully to others.**
> ... **Yes, God will give you much so that you can give away much . . . .**
>
> **II Corinthians 9:8, 11 *TLB***

Thoughts like this are not the thoughts of the natural man. Sad to say, they are not the thoughts of the average Christian either.

Remember how this relates to the fourth law of the harvest? The sower establishes the size of his harvest on the day he plants his seed. Second Corinthians 9:6 compares this principle to two farmers, one who plants much and one who plants little. The one who plants just a small amount of seed reaps only a small harvest. But the one who plants a large amount of seed reaps a very large harvest. Paul hereby emphasizes that the farmer who sows much seed positions himself for greater abundance than the one who plants little.

With this information, it is simple to conclude that the more you give to God, the more your return from God will be. If you give the amount God tells you to give (the tithe and generous offerings above the tithe), in time, you will have much more than you need. From that surplus you will be able to bless all the families of the earth. You will be able to feed them, clothe them, and above all, see to it that the Gospel of Jesus Christ is preached to them.

How much easier it is to be a blessing when you have planted much than when you have planted too little. Scant planting will bring about scant harvests. Shortsightedness in the time of sowing will place you in the uncomfortable position of short supply in the time of harvest. In shortage you will have to do without; you will have to borrow. You will not be able to be a blessing.

However, if your giving has been generous, your harvest will far exceed your needs. It is in abundance that your options are plentiful and pleasant. You can give some of the surplus to preach the Gospel to the lost; you can use some of the surplus to do the things you desire — take a vacation or attend that special conference.

In abundance, you have choices. In shortage, you have misery.

If you plant much, you can become one of those fortunate saints who has the problem of *budgeting your giving*.

By this, I mean determining what to do for God with your surplus money each month. If you plant little, you will become one of those unfortunate saints who has the problem of *budgeting your living*. That is, having to decide how to turn less than enough into barely enough.

I caution you, please don't let the devil deceive you into believing God doesn't want you to have surplus. God says just the opposite. He receives pleasure when you prosper.

> . . . **Let the Lord be magnified, which hath pleasure in the prosperity of his servant.**
> **Psalm 35:27**

It is obvious that it is easier to expand your activities to handle more than enough than it is to scale down your lifestyle to compensate for less than enough.

My wife and I have lived in both of these conditions. I can remember Christmases when we did not have nearly enough. How hard it was to stretch our few pennies to have at least a minimum number of inexpensive gifts for our five children. A few days before Christmas, we would bring out the meager gifts we had been able to purchase. I can remember us asking each other, "How will we ever make this be enough?" What heart-pain parents feel when there is not enough for their precious children!

There Is a Solution

Now that we have learned this simple law of the harvest, we sow (give) much so that we can reap (receive) much. How different Christmas gift giving is now. There is more than enough for everyone. When I say everyone, I mean a very large crowd of people — my wife, our five children, their spouses, their nine children, Pat's parents, my parents — and even enough for me to have nice gifts, too!

There has always been a surplus since we learned how to plant much and often. The Scripture is true. It works! God is not mocked. Whatsoever we sow, we reap. (Gal. 6:7.) The illustration of the Christmas gifts represents only a small part of the great blessing we have received from planting much.

The Spiritual Application

There is a spiritual application to this truth that is more devastating than not having enough Christmas gifts. When Christians position themselves in the torment of the insufficient harvest, they find themselves continuously having to say, "No!" to the Holy Spirit.

So many times in the early years of our marriage, my wife and I would sit in mission conferences listening to anointed speakers tell of the work of God in some distant land! How sorry we would be when God would impress us to give some large sum of money to that missionary only to realize that our funds (harvest) were too scarce to comply. This same painful thing happened each time our church would have a building program. How we wanted to give some special abundant gift to help! Again and again we had to say, "No," because our harvest was too small.

I can remember the early years of Trinity Broadcasting Network when we had to helplessly stand by and watch Paul and Jan Crouch struggling to make ends meet. I remember when their two boys were very young. The station was meagerly equipped. How our hearts burned to help them with some large cash gift — just to lift some of the burden from their shoulders — but our harvest was too small. I clearly remember the automobile they drove. It was an old gray, gasoline guzzling sedan that had long since seen its best days. How I wished I could buy them a nice new car, but I could only wish, because our harvest was too small.

My wife and I lived many years with the dissatisfaction of financial inability. Then God showed us from His Word that we could not wait until the time of need to decide how much seed to plant. We always had to plant our seed well in advance of our harvest. We had to plant as much as we could, even more than seemed reasonable to our natural minds. Only after doing this could we expect our harvest to meet all of our personal needs. Only then could we experience the surplus we needed to meet all the opportunities for giving that God presented.

Finally We Planted Enough Seed for a Proper Harvest

During these days of insufficiency, the church I was pastoring was entering a very large building program. At that time we were also selling our house to move closer to the new church location.

I was very excited about selling the old house and purchasing a new one. Our old home had appreciated tremendously. With its sale, we would have almost $40,000 for a down payment. This would mean we would only have to borrow half the cost of the new home.

Unexpectedly, God's Spirit spoke to me: "John, give me $10,000 from the house sale money. I want you to give it toward the building of the new church." I was so shocked, I almost cried. I must be honest. I had never before imagined being able to give this great an amount to God.

We had always been good givers. We wanted to give to God. We wanted to see the new church built. But we also wanted very much to own a house debt-free. How close we would be to our goal with the full $40,000 down payment. Why, with double payments, it would be paid off in less than 10 years. But God's will in the matter was overwhelming. He was revealing the fourth law of the harvest to us. Throughout the endless ages, my wife and I will thank God that we obeyed Him.

As my wife and I planted that $10,000 seed into our church, it was deemed to be a foolish move by the world's financial planners. But remember, they operate in the natural realm, for they do not recognize God's spiritual laws. Their knowledge of increasing finances operates in a technological mentality. The Christian's financial increase comes by way of an agricultural mentality.

Time and space do not allow for the entire story, but from that $10,000 seed has come a greater money harvest than I could ever have expected from the worldly financial system. Since that day, each of our harvests has been larger, and with each one, we have realized more surplus. This abundant planting continues to bring forth greater and greater harvests. It is of the utmost importance that you realize your harvest size is established when your seed is sown into the Gospel.

Faith Promise — A Biblical Way to a Greater Harvest

As you read the account of my house sale and subsequent gift of $10,000, you may be saying, "Well, that is well and good for you, Brother John, but I don't have a $40,000 equity from which to seed."

Dear friend, I did not have that kind of money to start with either. My wife and I started with $3.00 per week above our tithe of $4.00. This seems an insignificant amount according to today's standards, but I can remember when we made our faith-promise payments each week. The needs were so great that the temptation not to give the extra money to missions was tremendous. Stubbornly, though, we just kept on making those $3.00 mission payments throughout the year. Then the next year, we increased that amount to $5.00 per week.

Now think about it. A couple with four children living on $40.00 a week, raising their mission offering from $3.00 to $5.00 per week. Why, at the end of 52 weeks, we had given $260.00 to world missions. That equaled over five of our weekly paychecks. The $40,000.00 equity in our house was part of our harvest from previously planted seed.

Everyone Can Plant a Great Seed

Every one of you can start planting more by using the time-tested method of faith-promise giving. You don't have to wait until you have a financial windfall to give a substantial gift to God. Just set an amount that you can believe God for each week.

Let us suppose that you start with $10.00. Now that doesn't sound like much by itself, but when you multiply it times 52 weeks ($10 X 52) it equals $520.00 a year. Why, that's over half of $1,000.00. If you give $15.00 per week, it equals $780.00 a year. If you give $20.00 per week, it equals $1,040.00 each year, and so on.

With this in mind, contact your pastor, your Christian television network, or an evangelist God lays on your heart. Tell them you are going to give $520.00, and you will be paying it in 52 installments of $10.00. Believe me, they will be pleased to hear this.

Please don't be motivated to give *only* $10.00 per week because of this illustration. You may be able to give $40.00, $60.00, $100.00. Don't limit God. Multiply these amounts by 52 weeks, and you will be giving $2,080, $3,120, or $5,200 in a year. A faith promise will allow you to plant much more than you imagined possible.

Have Eyes To See Your Harvest

You must learn to look about you to identify God's increase. The harvest takes many forms. It could come in the form of automobile tires that last longer, utility bills that suddenly begin to decrease, better gas mileage on your car, children's shoes that last longer. All of these are part of your potential harvest.

There are more obvious ways to spot the signs of your increased harvest. A bit more overtime may come your way, or you might be offered a substantial price for some item that you thought to be of little value.

Keep an eye on the equity in your house. Many times people do not consider this as part of their harvest. Remember, the $10,000.00 that I gave to God from the equity of my home was the result of years of appreciation. Sometimes the increase takes the form of a notable miracle. When we sold our house, the realtor said he felt we received about $10,000.00 more than the house was worth.

Plant Your Seeds Abundantly
for a Bountiful Harvest

Make a quality decision. You must decide you will plant much so you can reap much. (II Cor. 9:6.) If you have some cash, get it together.

If you do not have any cash, consider an alternative. Sell something — a boat, a camper, a second automobile. Have a garage sale.

If these solutions do not fit your circumstances, make a faith promise to God. Determine an amount you will give faithfully each week. Do not make it an impossible amount, but also be careful not to make it an insignificant amount either. Remember, a faith promise is designed to stretch your faith to believe God for more seed. Always keep in mind that there is a thin line between faith and foolishness. If you have not been faithful in $50.00 per week, don't start with $200.00 per week.

Always ask the ministry you support to be in agreement with you — not just agreement that you will be able to give the promised money (seedtime), but also agreement that you will have an increased return (harvest). This was the standard operating procedure between the Apostle Paul and his donors. He clearly states the Philippians were not only in a giving (sowing) covenant with him, but they were also in a receiving (harvest) covenant with him.

> . . . ye Philippians know. . . that in the begin-
> ning of the gospel . . . no church communicated with
> me as concerning *giving and receiving,* but ye only.
> Philippians 4:15

Notice the next verse. The Philippians also seemed to have a faith-promise offering of some kind established with Paul, for they were giving to him regularly.

> . . . even in Thessalonica ye sent *once and again*
> unto my necessity.
> Philippians 4:16

Systematic, segmented giving is denoted here.

Your First Big Harvest
Will Bring Other Big Harvests

Whether the seed you sow comes from savings, the sale of some asset, from equity, or from the use of faith-promise giving, your harvest is guaranteed by God's Word.

> **God is able to make it up to you by giving you**
> *everything you need and more . . . .*
> **II Corinthians 9:8** *TLB*

Now that we have learned the fourth law of the harvest, we can confidently add it to our growing list. Let's quickly review.

Law #1: Your seed must be planted.
Law #2: You must render your seed useless.
Law #3: You must plant what you expect to harvest.
Law #4: Your harvest size is established when your seed is sown.

6

The Fifth Law of the Harvest:
Your Seed Must Be Planted in Good Ground

> But other (seed) fell into *good ground*, and brought forth . . . some an hundredfold, some sixtyfold, some thirtyfold.
>
> **Matthew 13:8**

The story of the sower planting his seed in four different kinds of ground is well known. This parable has multiple applications. The agricultural application is probably the easiest to understand. Seed spilled along the wayside and not covered over with earth is quickly eaten by birds. Seed sown into stony places without much depth of soil will spring up but soon wither from the hot sunshine. Seed sown among the thorns will eventually be choked and become unfruitful.

However, seed sown into good ground brings forth a miracle process of multiplication called the harvest. In harvest there will be some hundredfold increase, some sixtyfold increase, some thirtyfold increase.

Beyond the Agricultural Application

Jesus tells us there is much more to this parable than a mere lesson in agricultural increase.

> Hear ye (understand) **therefore the parable of the sower.**
>
> **Matthew 13:18**

Jesus now opens the hidden wisdom of the parable to His disciples. He tells us its primary application is planting His Gospel into the hearts of the lost world. Jesus parallels each illustration from the agricultural harvest with its counterpart in the spiritual harvest. The parallel lessons that can be drawn from this parable are endless. However, let us go quickly to the application that shows us how to reap the hundredfold, sixtyfold, and thirtyfold financial harvest.

Only when we sow our seed into the good ground does it produce the optimum harvest. From this parable we can conclude that bad or mediocre ground will not bring forth any harvest at all.

If, as Jesus said, only the good ground produces the abundant agricultural harvest, and if only the good ground produces an abundant spiritual harvest, it is obvious that only the good ground will produce the abundant financial harvest.

The Good Ground for Finances

In the Gospel of Mark we are told that by giving our offerings into the Kingdom of God (the good ground), we have the potential of a one hundredfold financial increase. Be careful to note that Jesus does not say this hundredfold increase is collected after death. He emphasizes that it takes place *now in this present world.*

> ... There is no man that hath left house ... or lands, for my sake, and the gospel's,
> But he shall receive an hundredfold *now in this time*, houses ... and lands ....
> **Mark 10:29, 30**

The spiritual benefit of planting your seed in good ground is everlasting life. It is understood by all that our greatest spiritual harvest comes after physical death.

> **. . . and in the world to come eternal life.**
> **Mark 10:30**

Every person knows we will have no use for money in heaven. There will be no rent on our dwelling places. There will be no utility bills.

What is not so universally understood is if there is ever to be a financial increase from God, it must be given to us here on planet Earth. Money is only of use to us while we are still alive. Jesus said we will receive an hundredfold increase of houses and lands *now in this time.*

Parallel Harvest Principles Abound in Scripture

Notice how Jesus parallels the one who gives houses and lands, things that can be measured in a dollar value (Mark 10:29, 30), with the one who sows seed into the good ground (Matthew 13:8). He promises the one hundredfold increase to both. The law of the harvest operates in both realms, the agricultural as well as the financial. Multiplication of both harvests appears throughout the Bible.

> **Give, and it shall be given unto you; good**
> **measure, pressed down, and shaken together, and**
> **running over, shall men give into your bosom . . . .**
> **Luke 6:38**

> ... Jesus answered and said, Verily I say unto
> you, There is no man that hath left house ... or lands,
> for my sake, and the gospel's, But he shall receive an
> hundredfold now in this time, houses ... and lands.
> **Mark 10:29, 30**

> Verily, verily, I say unto you, Except a corn of
> wheat fall into the ground and die, it abideth alone:
> but if it die, it bringeth forth much fruit.
> **John 12:24**

> He that goeth forth and weepeth, bearing
> precious seed, shall doubtless come again with re-
> joicing, bringing his sheaves (the harvest) with him.
> **Psalm 126:6**

Each of these verses clearly states the eternal purpose of God to multiply seed sown into good ground by bringing forth a harvest.

Every Ministry Is Not Good Ground

I thank God for every good, Gospel-preaching ministry and every local church that operates in the earth today. However, you and I both know that not all ministries and churches preach the full Gospel. By this we can conclude that not all ministries and churches are good ground.

The next four sentences are extremely important; read them carefully.

There are ministries and churches that *exist* to minister. On the other hand, there are also ministries and churches that *minister* to exist. One raises money to minister. The other ministers to raise money.

There is an unmistakable characteristic that exists in every good-ground ministry. It will vigorously attempt to accomplish the specific purpose given to it by God. This is the true sign of a good-ground ministry.

Direct salvation of souls is not always the God-given purpose of every true ministry. I have long been associated with Trinity Broadcasting Network. Their God-directed purpose is to preach the Gospel of Jesus Christ to the whole world by way of electronic media (television and radio). There is no question that TBN wins souls every day, but that is not the primary evidence that identifies it as good ground.

For instance, suppose TBN acquired a license to build a television station in a Moslem nation. Suppose they faithfully preached Christ to that nation for several years. What if, at the end of that time, not one person had been saved? Would we then have to conclude that TBN was not a good-ground ministry? Of course not, for their commission from God is to preach Christ to all the world by way of electronic media.

The salvation of souls by any ministry is a wonderful sign, but it is not the final proof that your financial seed will be multiplied in that ministry. Remember the Apostle Paul's words.

> **I have planted, Apollos watered; but *God* gave the increase.**
> **I Corinthians 3:6**

The one who plants cannot save a soul. Likewise, the one who waters cannot save a soul. Only Jesus, the Lord of the harvest, can save a soul. The planter is a good-ground ministry *if* he was sent to *plant*. The one who waters is a good-ground ministry if God has instructed him to *water*.

Suppose some local church grew exceedingly fast, only to have the pastor realize that too many of the precious converts were returning to the world. That pastor might be led by the Lord to de-emphasize soul winning for a season and concentrate on bringing the new converts into greater Christian maturity. Even though the church might slow its explosive growth, it would not mean the church had ceased to be good ground. Every church is commissioned by God to bring forth fruit. Every church is also commissioned to see that the fruit it produces *remains*.

There are ministries that show impressive altar results which, upon close observation, would be found to be poor ground. These ministries might generate a massive show of hands to the question, "Will you accept Christ as Savior?" But after salvation, they may just leave those souls unattended.

There are other ministries that may not see nearly as many hands raised to the question, "Who wants to be saved?" However, they may see to it that almost all who do respond follow the Lord in baptism, then into the full assurance of their salvation and the filling of the Holy Spirit. They may continue until they have seen their converts into productive Christian lives. This is more likely to be good ground than the ministry that merely has a great show of hands.

Use Your Unction

God has given each Christian an unction.

> . . . ye have an *unction* from the Holy One, and
> ye know all things.
> 1 John 2:20

With your God-given unction you can discern the good ground. For several years, my wife and I supported a ministry that was reaching a particularly needy segment of the population. They faithfully witnessed Christ as they rendered their services. We gave generously and regularly to their support.

One day my wife became uneasy about writing the monthly check for this organization. This was her unction (discernment) operating. She felt in her spirit that something in this ministry had significantly changed. With this warning sign we did some investigation.

Do No Be Afraid To Investigate

We soon found that this ministry had abandoned the good work they were called to and had gone into a totally different ministry. This new realm of ministry, while biblical, was greatly duplicated by others. They had abandoned the ministry of their *calling* and inaugurated the ministry of their *choosing*. We determined to stop planting our financial seed with them because we felt they had left their God-given purpose.

Now hear this. The new direction of this ministry won more souls. To do so, however, they had to leave the ministry God impressed us to support them in. We had to conclude that while they were fine folks, their ministry was no longer good ground for us. It was no longer the ground that would bring us the hundredfold, sixtyfold, or thirtyfold increase.

Your Full-Gospel Church Is Good Ground

Any local church that teaches, preaches, and practices the full truth of God is always good ground. Pay close attention to what I just said, for not every local church preaches the full truth.

Some become social clubs or evolve into private "bless-me" clubs. However, local churches that preach the full Gospel, obeying the great commission to go into all the earth and preach the Gospel, are good ground. When you plant your finances in this kind of church, you can expect the hundredfold, sixtyfold, and thirtyfold increase from God.

If you give your hard-earned money to a church that does not fit the above description, do not expect a harvest. You may be a member of a church because of its convenient location or because of your ancestral ties, but remember, your seed must be planted in good ground if you want a harvest. If you are in a church that is poor ground, my advice to you is to get out of it *now!* Get into a proper church. Even if the building is not as nice or the church is not as prestigious, get into a full-gospel church that is good ground.

Ministries That Honor the Local Church Are Good Ground

There are many para-church ministries (ministries that work parallel to the local church). Many of these make excellent ground for planting your financial seed. These special ministries effectively preach the Gospel world-wide, conducting crusades, schools, seminars, and special meetings. Many times they are able to minister to portions of the world's population that are extremely difficult, if not impossible, for the average local church to reach.

A few examples of good-ground para-church ministries are those who minister to prisoners, retarded persons, military personnel, refugees, disaster victims, homosexuals, members of violent gangs, minority groups, people in remote regions of the earth, etc. All of these are vital to the Gospel. Many of these are God-ordained ministries. They must be supported, but they should meet some specific qualifications before you consider them to be good ground.

Whenever possible, they should have a good working relationship with the local church. Above all else, let me repeat, they should primarily exist to accomplish their God-given calling.

If they are called to feed the hungry, they should receive your finances in order to feed hungry people. They should not feed hungry people in order to receive your finances. If their purpose is to clothe the naked, they should not just collect and distribute pictures of needy people. They should primarily provide clothing for the needy. If a ministry is called to minister to prisoners, their primary expenditure should be for preaching the Gospel to prisoners.

Evangelistic organizations should raise money to hold evangelistic crusades. They should not operate in the manner that one evangelist's television director described to me. He said the well-known evangelist he represented had not held a crusade in over six years. All his weekly television programs were edited re-runs of past meetings. This evangelist's primary purpose was to raise funds from Christians who were being misled into believing he was still holding crusades every month. His ministry is not good ground.

Good-Ground Ministries
Are Open for Inspection

Before you can classify a ministry as good ground, you must have more information about it than just what you read in its financial appeal letters. Ask some questions of the ministry you support. Go to their meetings occasionally. I know for a fact that the real God-ordained ministries welcome your inquiries about their operations.

Go to Tulsa and visit Oral Roberts University. While in the area, stop in and see Kenneth Hagin's Rhema Bible Training Center. These men have nothing to hide. Attend one of R.W. Schambach's crusades. He will be delighted to have you present. Plan to go with Morris Cerullo to a foreign field. See the great work God does through him among the nations of the world. Drop in on a church in your area where Dwight Thompson is ministering. He will welcome your visit, and it will be a blessing to you. Be at Crenshaw Christian Center on a Sunday morning and verify for yourself the great work Dr. Frederick K.C. Price is doing.

Please do not think this short list represents all the good-ground ministries. There are hundreds of other men and women of God whose ministries qualify.

Christian Television Stations

I am associated with many wonderful Christian television stations across America. These are very special end-time ministries. They are unique in that they serve in a different way from para-church ministries. They do not operate parallel with the church, but true Christian television stations operate primarily as an *extension* of the local church.

Most Christian television stations are not the ministry of one individual. They are an extension of many local churches to the area they serve. They also extend the ministry of Bible teachers and evangelists into private homes, hotels, bars, prisons, etc. Wherever television sets exist, these stations send the message of the church beyond its four walls into the habitat of man. They take the message of the church where the people are.

Christian television stations are among the best ground available to Christians today. However, please take the time to verify the ministry of any station you support. Ask some pointed questions. I have never known of a Christian television station that would not cheerfully discuss the station's philosophy of outreach and results with any serious inquirer. I have never heard of one station that did not enjoy visitors, especially as a part of the live audience during appropriate programs.

Make it a point to visit one of the great Christian television stations in a city on your vacation route this year. I know you will be welcomed.

The Responsibility of Choosing the Good Ground

Don't let the few impostors (bad-ground ministries) keep you from enjoying the benefits of the good ground. God does not leave you on your own when it comes to choosing the place to plant your financial seed. He is willing to direct you. Just ask Him. He will lead you in your giving by burdening your heart for specific ministries and projects. Just be sure to do your part when you feel God's leading.

1. Use your Holy Ghost-given unction.
2. Use your good common sense.
3. Care enough to investigate.

Investigate, Then Invest.

God will lead you where the hundredfold, sixtyfold, and thirtyfold harvest will come. Remember, you can only experience harvest when your seed is planted in good ground. See how our list of God's laws of the harvest is increasing with each chapter. Let us quickly review those we have already covered, and add this new one.

Law #1: Your seed must be planted.
Law #2: You must render your seed useless.
Law #3: You must plant what you expect to harvest.
Law #4: Your harvest size is established when your seed is sown.
Law #5: Your seed must be planted in good ground.

7

The Sixth Law of the Harvest:
You Must Always Wait
a Period of Time
Between Planting and Harvesting

. . . a man should cast a seed into the ground;
And should sleep, and rise night and day, and
the seed should spring and grow up . . . .
Mark 4:26, 27

Thank God for the ministry of the faith teachers in recent years. How far forward these anointed men of God have brought the Church since the mid 1960's!

Those of you who can remember the prevailing theology before that time will recall it was common to blame God for every misfortune that befell the Church or its members. The error of that day caused us to believe cancer was one of God's ways of calling His precious saints home. We even believed God would cause the death of a child to get the attention of an erring parent. How nice it is to now know God is always on our side. He is not the author of our tragedies.

The children of God have learned a great deal from the faith teachers. But the faith message must be extended to emphasize *patience*. Realize that I am not saying we need a message to replace the faith message, but a message to complete it. The expanded message of patience is the scriptural succession to the faith message. In the Bible we read it is not through faith alone that we receive the promise, but it is through *faith* and through *patience*.

81

> ... be not slothful, but followers of them who
> through faith and *patience* inherit the promises.
> Hebrews 6:12

To My Knowledge, Only One Harvest Comes Without Patience

Let me clarify this statement. In the regular course of preaching the above text, I used to say there was nothing under the sun that produced an instantaneous harvest. I felt very safe in this and emphasized it with several illustrations — corn, wheat, apples, acorns, and so on.

After one particular service, I was at the altar shaking hands with some of the church members when a precious saint came to me. She said if it would not be taken as a rebuke, she would like to correct a statement I had made. I responded that if she would just be gentle, I believed I would be able to stand correction without letting it ruin the rest of my day.

With this said, she gave me a big smile. I smiled back at her and said, "Well, let's have it. I'm ready. What did I say wrong this morning?" She smiled again, a sweet and loving smile. I smiled back even broader and said, "O.K. What is it? What did I get wrong?"

She said, "There is one thing you can give away and receive from it an instantaneous harvest."

I asked her to please tell me what it was, because for the life of me, I could not think of one single thing. She smiled even broader this time and just held the smile on her face.

I must say, I was growing a bit impatient. People were standing behind her waiting to shake hands with me. No matter, she just stood there. As I looked into her friendly, smiling face, I couldn't help but forget my impatience with her, and I just smiled back at her, bigger than ever.

I took her by the hands and said, "All right. Now tell me. What is it you can plant that immediately comes back to you in a harvest?"

She answered, "*A nice, big smile!* As soon as you give it away, it comes right back to you." She had just planted three great, big smiles on me, and even in my impatience, I had immediately given a harvest of smiles back to her.

Since that day, I have used this illustration throughout the world. I have had people of many nations look about the room and quickly give a smile to someone nearby. Well, I must report that the dear woman was right. It works in Africa. It works in America. It works in England. It works in Asia. It works in Mexico. It works in South America. It works in Italy. In fact, I have never seen it operate differently than she said it would.

There Is a Time of Waiting

There is a Scripture that is very popular. It is even used in secular realms. It is usually quoted in this way. "Cast your bread upon the water, and it will come back to you again."

While this rendition of the verse gives the essence of the truth in giving and receiving, it leaves out one of the essentials of the harvest. As just quoted, it does not teach the necessity of having patience between casting your bread upon the water and the time it takes to come back to you.

Look at the verse in its fullness as it appears in the Scriptures. You will immediately see that God emphasizes the necessity of patience between the time of sowing and the time of reaping. He inspired Solomon to write this verse in such a way that patience is shown to be a law of the harvest.

> **Cast thy bread upon the waters: for thou shalt find it** *after many days.*
>
> **Ecclesiastes 11:1**

This is nothing more than an expansion of the "golden rule".

The "Golden Rule" Operates on Faith and Patience

The "golden rule" is one of those truths from Scripture that is so dynamic, it is not only popular with those who believe the Bible; it is also popular with non-believers. Throughout the world, you will find this great truth from God's Word repeated. You will see it on greeting cards, on billboards, and so on.

> **. . . all things whatsoever ye would that men should do to you, do ye even so to them: for this is the law and the prophets.**
>
> **Matthew 7:12**

There is, however, a waiting period between "doing unto others" before it will be "done again unto you."

Please allow me another personal illustration. A few years ago when my wife and I pastored, we gave ourselves totally to a hand- picked group of elders. They received from us everything we had to give. They were given our time, our knowledge, our finances — our very lives.

Then came the time when God said we would depart from that church for a season. We left with confidence, feeling that since we had given, we would now receive back from them all the love and support we had sown into their lives.

Well, much to our surprise, they immediately began to treat us as total strangers. They quickly separated themselves from us, leaving us bewildered. Our hearts were broken. Satan used this unchristian attitude to challenge the very validity of the "golden rule." We had given all we had, and received the cold shoulder in return.

How much easier this would have been to bear if we had really understood the sixth law of the harvest. We would not reap immediately upon sowing. Our bread had been cast upon the water, but now we had to wait the "many days" of Ecclesiastes 11:1.

Doubts, fears, disappointments, and feelings of betrayal haunted us night and day. This tragedy was about to take us under when this precious sixth law of the harvest was made real to us. Little by little, we began to understand there will always be a time of waiting between sowing our seed and reaping our harvest.

Now, after almost six years, my wife and I are seeing our bread of kindness and love coming back on every wave. The benefits pour in daily from literally hundreds of folks from around the world. Many new friends have come into our lives and lavish us with the standard of love and respect we planted in the lives of those elders. By experience, we now know not to look for our harvest on the same day we sow our seed.

Scriptures on Patience Abound

Notice how important patience is to harvesting the promise of God.

> . . . the good ground are they, which in an honest and good heart, having heard the word, keep it, and bring forth fruit with *patience*.
>> **Luke 8:15**

> . . . if we hope for that we see not, then do we with *patience* wait for it.
>> **Romans 8:25**

> . . . ye have need of *patience*, that, after ye have done the will of God, ye might receive the promise.
>> **Hebrews 10:36**

> . . . be not slothful, but followers (imitators) of them who through faith and *patience* inherit the promises.
>> **Hebrews 6:12**

> . . . after he (Abraham) had *patiently* endured, he obtained the promise.
>> **Hebrews 6:15**

Each of these Scriptures has two things in common. First, each speaks of *patience*. Secondly, each verse promises that those who patiently wait (allow time to pass) *receive* the thing they wait for.

Impatience Will Cancel Your Harvest

How can a financial harvest be canceled? It can easily be done by the one who plants the seed.

Let me begin by explaining the world's financial system. Suppose you go to the bank and plant $1,000 into a five-year Certificate of Deposit at an interest rate of 10% per year. If you patiently leave the CD undisturbed for five years, it will pay you the $1,000.00 you initially invested, plus your interest at 10% compounded over the five-year period.

However, if for some reason you become impatient and demand the money back before the maturity date — if your impatience causes you to disturb it even one day short of the full five years — you will forfeit the harvest on your investment. You will not get one cent of interest (harvest) on your $1,000.00, and under certain circumstances, you can even lose a substantial portion of your original investment.

The natural realm responds to impatience with cancellation of the harvest!

First the Natural, Then the Supernatural

Impatience causes the same thing to happen in the realm of biblical economics. If you plant a $1,000.00 seed into the gospel ministry, you must not allow yourself to become impatient. While waiting for the manifestation of your harvest, do not begin to murmur and complain. If you begin to say things like, "God's plan of financial harvest does not work. I don't think God will come through this time. I have waited long enough," you will immediately cancel your harvest.

Notice that I said immediately! There is something you must realize when you follow God into the financial harvest. You must remember that you are leaving the realm of the natural and entering the realm of the *supernatural.*

In the natural realm, you can say that your CD is not going to pay you any increase, but as long as you do not alter the written terms, it will still fund as promised when the date of maturity arrives. Men cannot see the hearts and intentions of other men in the natural realm, so they must rely on written statements. Only when the written document is canceled in writing is your natural harvest canceled.

In the spiritual realm, there is a superior principle at work. Things are much more finely tuned. Everything can change in a moment with just a few words, be they words of faith or words of doubt. In this superior realm, words are very powerful.

A lifetime of crime and sin cannot be done away with in the natural courts by simply saying you are sorry, but in the spiritual world it can be completely and eternally eliminated by saying, "Oh, God, be merciful to me, a sinner." Those few words, in the supernatural, spirit realm, make every sin as if it had never happened. God looks upon the heart and knows our thoughts and intentions.

> For verily I say unto you, That whosoever shall
> *say* unto this mountain, Be thou removed, and be
> thou cast into the sea; and shall *not doubt in his heart*,
> but shall *believe* that those things which he *saith*
> shall come to pass, *he shall have whatsoever he saith.*
> **Mark 11:23**

I am convinced that Christians have missed some of the greatest financial harvests of all time. They simply spoke them out of existence from hearts of impatience. How many times I have heard well-meaning people speak away their harvest — even after they have invested their hard-earned money into good-ground ministries! They cancel it all by simply making some dumb statement like, "Well, I guess faith-giving doesn't work. I planted my seed in the Gospel, and it looks like nothing is going to happen."

In essence, they are saying, "I cancel my harvest."

> . . .he shall have whatsoever he saith.
> **Mark 11:23**

Keep Faith; Be Patient; the Harvest Is Coming

> . . . let us not be weary in well doing: for in due
> season *we shall reap, if we faint not.*
> **Galatians 6:9**

How quickly some of us faint! We determine to give to God's work, but many times the ink is not dry on the check before our old enemy, *impatience*, moves in and initiates the cancellation order.

Just settle down! Reject that which challenges God's Word. Whatever you do, do not become *impatient*. Make up your mind not to allow your mouth to stop your harvest. God says your harvest will come if you planted in *faith* and stand in *patience*.

> **Casting down imaginations, and every high thing that exalteth itself against the knowledge of God, and bringing into captivity every thought to the obedience of Christ.**
> **II Corinthians 10:5**

Keep on believing God until your harvest comes in. Let *patience* take your faith to its full potential. In the end, you will have the victory. You will reap the harvest you planted.

> **. . . take unto you the whole armour of God, that ye may be able to withstand in the evil day, and having done all, to stand. Stand, therefore . . . .**
> **Ephesians 6:13, 14**

When you have done all God has instructed you to do, just stand there until your harvest is *in your hand*.

In the Spirit Realm the Rewards Are Greater

Remember that although it takes more discipline to have a harvest in the spiritual realm, the harvest will always be greater than it will be in the natural. In the natural realm, a financial harvest of 10% to 20% is considered extremely good. However, the smallest harvest in the spiritual realm begins at thirtyfold (30 times) and progresses up to one hundredfold (100 times).

Impatience arises when we do not believe God. We think God will not supply, or He will not supply on time. If you just think about it, *patience* is the battery that runs the clock of *faith*. As long as you believe God, the battery will run the clock. The day *patience* dies, *faith* stops, and your harvest is canceled.

Law #1: Your seed must be planted.

Law #2: You must render your seed useless.

Law #3: You must plant what you expect to harvest.

Law #4: Your harvest size is established when your seed is sown.

Law #5: Your seed must be planted in good ground.

Law #6: You must always wait a period of time between planting and harvesting.

8

The Seventh Law of the Harvest:
You Must Maintain Your Crops for a Proper Harvest

. . . the thorns sprung up, and choked them. . . .

Matthew 13:7

Proper maintenance is essential to a proper harvest. Seed will become unfruitful if left to the ravages of a hostile environment. Insects are very destructive to the growth of the farmer's crop. They eat the lush leaves. They destroy the precious grain. Left unchecked, they will soon render the best of crops unfruitful.

Weeds also cause damage to the crop. They compete with the seed for the precious nutrition of the ground. Anything that takes the ground's nourishment from the crop will eventually render it unfruitful. Vermin will eat the stalks and leaves, preventing the farmer from enjoying a bountiful harvest.

All the destructive enemies of the harvest just mentioned can be controlled if the farmer follows proper maintenance procedures.

It is obvious it would be more convenient for the farmer to do nothing toward the maintenance of his crop. It would be easier to follow some interesting course of action instead — maybe sports or some form of recreation. The farmer might like to enjoy a time of leisure while the seed is growing.

However, if he does not maintain his crop, he will not have the privilege of a harvest. Insects must be controlled. Weeds must be kept to a minimum. Vermin must be stopped at any cost.

If proper maintenance procedures are faithfully executed, they will keep the farmer busy from the day he plants until the harvest is completed. The successful farmer has to work hard and long to care for his crop and fields. His labor assures him of an optimum harvest.

Proper Maintenance of the Financial Harvest

There are three areas of maintenance you cannot overlook if you expect to receive an abundant financial harvest.

1. *You must put God and a Godly lifestyle first!*

> ... seek ye *first* the kingdom of God, and his righteousness; and all these things shall be added unto you.
> **Matthew 6:33**

This verse of Scripture is vital to those who plan to participate in God's financial harvest. If you follow its instructions, God will add to you *everything* necessary to a successful life — food, lodging, clothing, retirement, and life's comforts.

When Jesus said, *"all these things,"* He spoke of material goods. However, notice the two qualifications for receiving them are spiritual.

First, He says we must seek the Kingdom of God before anything else. How confusing this statement can become, especially when you consider all the contradictory teaching about the Kingdom of God that exists today. The doctrines are many. Some teach *Kingdom now*, others the *invisible Kingdom*, and yet another group only sees the Kingdom as the millennial reign of Christ. My, how men can make the Word of God seem so confusing.

When Jesus said to seek first the Kingdom of God, He did not intend to stir a doctrinal controversy. He simply meant we should strive, above all else, to *allow* the Kingdom of God to manifest itself in us.

The Kingdom of God Is in You

The Kingdom of God is like any other kingdom in this particular aspect. It is the place where a king reigns (rules). In the kingdom of England, the monarch of England rules. The kingdom of Monaco is where the King of Monaco reigns. In the kingdom of darkness, the devil reigns.

The Kingdom of God is simply where God, Jehovah, and His Son, Jesus Christ, reign. The Kingdom of God also differs from the kingdoms of the world in a unique way.

Every kingdom of the world is a geographic kingdom. It has tangible borders. But the Kingdom of God does not have geographic (tangible) borders. It is a spiritual kingdom. The Apostle Paul describes it as a kingdom that is in men.

> **For the kingdom of God is not meat and drink (tangible); but righteousness, and peace, and joy in the Holy Ghost (spiritual).**
> **Romans 14:17**

Seeking first the Kingdom of God is the process of actively seeking the rulership of Jesus Christ in your life. To do this you must dethrone the devil. Then you must invite Jesus Christ to take His place on the throne of your life. You must replace your own will, and the will of others, with His will. All usurpers are to be thrown down, and Jesus is to be set up as the absolute ruler of your life.

The Righteousness of God

This is the second qualification you must fulfill to have "all these things" added to your life. *You must seek His righteousness as vigorously as you seek His Kingdom.*

Teachings on the righteousness of God have brought the Church a mixed blessing. The confusion comes primarily from what men have taught the righteousness of God to be. There are many *man-made* rules of righteousness. They range from dress codes, to rigorous prayer schedules, to unattainable rules of abstinence, and beyond.

God's righteousness does not consist of a set of man's rules. To seek God's righteousness, first of all, you must be saved. When you accept Jesus and His substitutionary atonement, this imparts to you the very righteousness of God.

> ... that I may win Christ,
> And be found in him, not having mine own righteousness, which is of the law, but that which is through the faith of Christ, the righteousness which is of God by faith.
>
> **Philippians 3:8, 9**

After being saved, seeking His righteousness goes beyond this initial *provisional* righteousness. God desires that we continue on into the *practical* righteousness of God. We do this by pressing toward the goal of actually becoming like Jesus Christ.

> . . . we all, with open face beholding as in a glass the glory of the Lord, are changed into the same image from glory to glory, even as by the Spirit of the Lord.
>
> II Corinthians 3:18

Please notice that of these two qualifications, neither is meant to be more important than the other. Seeking the Kingdom of God and seeking the righteousness of God are both essential to your financial harvest. Jesus said if we are not first seeking to expand these two dimensions of our lives, we are not going to receive "all these things" from Him.

A very important part of your financial harvest is accomplished by properly maintaining your relationship with God. Without daily care of this relationship, you block the possibility of receiving the increase you desire. You must realize that even seed sown in good ground is at risk if your life is void of spiritual growth and substance.

> . . . seek ye first the kingdom of God, and His righteousness; and all these things shall be added unto you.
>
> Matthew 6:33

2. *The evangelization of the world must be a priority.*

> . . . remember the Lord thy God: for it is he that giveth thee power to get wealth, that he may

establish his covenant which he sware unto thy fathers, as it is this day.
Deuteronomy 8:18

This verse tells us we have been given the supernatural power to get wealth. It also clearly states the specific purpose for giving us this power. It is to establish the covenant God made with our fathers, Abraham, Isaac, and Jacob.

We Are Not the Seed of Moses

This covenant between God and Abraham is not well understood by the children of God. I find that most of the Church tends to confuse it with the covenant God made with natural Israel.

In Deuteronomy 28, the Lord gave a covenant to natural Israel through Moses. Obedient Israelites would be greatly blessed, and disobedient Israelites would be left exposed to the curse.

We must always remember that there was not only a covenant made with Abraham's natural seed, Israel. There was also a covenant made with his spiritual seed, spiritual Israel, the Church. Every Christian is included in the spiritual seed of Abraham.

. . . if ye be Christ's, then are ye Abraham's seed, and heirs according to the promise.
Galatians 3:29

There is a significant difference between the covenants made with these two Israels. The covenant presented by

Moses promised to bless those who complied with the commandments. Notice how its motivation appealed to the human nature by making promises of *being blessed.*

The covenant with Abraham's spiritual seed appeals to something much greater in its recipients. It appeals to the divine nature — the nature that only exists in those who have been born again. That nature is like the nature of Jesus Christ who was not on the earth seeking to *be blessed,* but His motivation was to *be a blessing.*

> ... I will make of thee a great nation, and I will bless thee, and make thy name great; and *thou shalt be a blessing:*
> And I will bless them that bless thee, and curse him that curseth thee: and *in thee shall all families of the earth be blessed.*
> **Genesis 12:2, 3**

The power to get wealth is explicitly promised to those who desire to *be a blessing* instead of only wishing *to be blessed.* It is a promise made exclusively to those who will bless the world. They will do this with the Gospel of Jesus Christ by meeting the needs of the hungry, the naked, and the homeless.

You, spiritual Israel, have been given supernatural, miracle power to get wealth so you can be a blessing.

Obtaining Wealth Is Essential to the Great Commission

In the first chapter of Acts, Jesus made a powerful statement.

99

> ... ye shall receive power, after that the Holy
> Ghost is come upon you: and ye shall be witnesses
> unto me both in Jerusalem, and in all Judea, and in
> Samaria, and unto the uttermost part of the earth.
> **Acts 1:8**

Jesus told you to be a faithful witness in your Jerusalem, your Judea, your Samaria and the uttermost parts of the world. To do this, you must walk in abundance. You must have the money to send others to the places you are not able to go.

The word *power* literally means ability. God will give you the unique ability to do this. Don't despair. Remember, you are the seed of Abraham.

> ... if ye be Christ's, then are ye Abraham's
> seed, and heirs according to the promise.
> **Galatians 3:29**

You are the heir of the promises. God will give your hands the same power to get wealth that He gave to Abraham. He will fund the covenant He made to enable you to be a blessing in Jerusalem, Judea, Samaria, and even to the uttermost parts of the world.

You can more easily do this today than ever before through giving to your local church, Christian television station, favorite evangelist or teacher. Remember, God has given you power to get wealth so His covenant of blessing can be established in and through you.

God will increase your harvest if your intentions are proper. Proper intentions go beyond just blessing yourself.

He will supply you the wealth when your intention is to *be a blessing.*

3. *You must discern deception.*

The devil possesses three basic powers — the power to tempt, the power to accuse, and the power to deceive. Of these three powers, deceit is the hardest to defend yourself against.

The power to tempt can be overcome by seeking God's promised way of escape.

> **There hath no temptation taken you but such as is common to man: but God is faithful, who will not suffer you to be tempted above that ye are able; but will, with the temptation also make a way to escape, that ye may be able to bear it.**
> **I Corinthians 10:13**

The power to accuse can cause even the strongest to fall, but it can be easily overcome by knowing who you are in Christ. You are the righteousness of God in Christ. (II Cor. 5:21.) You are a royal ambassador sent from God. (II Cor. 5:20.) You are filled with the Father, Son, and Holy Spirit.

> **. . . greater is he** (Jesus) **that is in you, than he** (the devil) **that is in the world.**
> **1 John 4:4**

The most dangerous power the devil has in his arsenal is the power of deception.

> **. . . that old serpent, called the Devil, and Satan, which deceiveth the whole world . . . .**
> **Revelation 12:9**

101

> . . . if it were possible, they shall deceive the
> very elect.
>
> **Matthew 24:24**

Deception is devastating! In the parable of the sower we saw that the deceitfulness of riches causes men to become unfruitful. (Matt. 13:22.) When your financial harvest begins, do not be deceived by the expansion of your wealth. Do not begin to lavish it upon yourself. Remember these words:

> Ye ask, and *receive not*, because ye ask amiss,
> that ye may *consume it upon your lusts*.
> **James 4:3**

Being deceived by the sudden influx of wealth will turn the harvest process around. This deception will quickly cause you to become unfruitful.

> . . . the *deceitfulness* of riches, choke the word,
> and *he becometh unfruitful*.
> **Matthew 13:22**

You must maintain a clean, godly life, always moving nearer to God. Give the lion's share of your surplus to the evangelization of the world. Scripture tells us to properly maintain even the smallest part of our lives in holiness, for even small intrusions and violations can destroy your entire harvest.

> . . . the little foxes . . . spoil the vines . . . .
> **Song of Solomon 2:15**

Uncontrolled sin is like the foxes of the field. It will spoil even the finest harvest.

Properly maintained crops bring forth abundant harvests. Rehearse with me again the laws of the harvest we have learned to this point.

Law #1: Your seed must be planted.

Law #2: You must render your seed useless.

Law #3: You must plant what you expect to harvest.

Law #4: Your harvest size is established when your seed is sown.

Law #5: Your seed must be planted in good ground.

Law #6: You must always wait a period of time between planting and harvesting.

Law #7: You must maintain your crops for a proper harvest.

9

The Eighth Law of the Harvest:
You Must Always Sow
To Your Harvest Size,
Not From Your Harvest Size

. . . Isaac sowed in that land (of famine)**, and
received in the same year an hundredfold . . . .**
Genesis 26:12

I have never lived on a farm, so everything I learned
about farming was new to me. Not too long ago, I learned
something that came as quite a surprise. The time when a
farmer must make his largest seed purchase is when he can
least afford it. This happens when he has suffered a previous
crop failure. During this time, funds are very short. The
pressure to conserve is great. The farmer is in a dilemma, for
he must plant more seed than ever in order to make up for the
shortage caused by the failed crop.

When this situation occurs, he must plow up the fallow
ground, the part of the farm that goes uncultivated each year.
He must even lease additional land. If he does not have
enough cash for this untimely expense, he must borrow. The
farmer must do all he can to plant as many acres of seed as
possible. The time he needs his biggest harvest is always the
time when his funds are the shortest.

Wise farmers always plant *to* their harvest. They never
limit the amount of seed they plant because of the previous
year's crop failure.

105

Farmers Have Taught Me Much

This truth was pointed out to me by a Colorado farmer named Clint Newman. Clint was one of our nation's largest wheat farmers, planting thousands of acres each year. I thank God for the many things this faithful saint of God taught me.

Time after time, farmers have taught me great truths from God's Word. I am grateful for their input into my life, for I can now share much of this information with you.

Several years ago, I ministered in a very small town in Kansas. The entire population was made up of farmers. During a question-and-answer period, I asked them if they understood that the laws of the financial harvest were parallel with the laws governing their agricultural harvest. They quickly acknowledged that they knew this truth.

With this response, I almost decided not to teach that subject. But as hard as I tried not to, the Holy Ghost would not allow me to teach anything else. Reluctantly, I began teaching the laws of the harvest.

I must admit, I felt foolish as I taught them that "a seed must be planted," and "you must plant what you expect to harvest," and so on. One by one, I continued to teach these principles, until I came to the eighth law: "sow *to* your harvest, not *from* your harvest."

Suddenly, these veteran farmers began to look around at each other with puzzled expressions. I sensed that something was very wrong and asked, "Gentlemen, have I taught something you disagree with?"

I actually got a lump in my throat as I awaited their response. After all, these men were all experts on the subject. Here I was, a city boy, teaching seasoned farmers the laws of the harvest.

For a moment, no one answered. Finally, one of them spoke up. He said, "Brother John, you are absolutely right. Every farmer knows you must always sow *to* your desired harvest size. When a farmer can least afford it, he must sow the greatest amount of seed. Even if a failed harvest has left him almost bankrupt, he must plant more the next time.

"The thing that has impacted me is that while I faithfully adhere to this principle in my agricultural harvest, I have never applied this law to my financial harvest. I have been sowing *from* my financial harvests, not *to* my financial harvests."

All the farmers in the room agreed that when their crops provided good income, they would give large amounts to God's work. However, when crops failed, and income was low, they gave very little into the Gospel. They all faithfully applied the eighth law of the harvest to their agricultural farms, but not one of them was applying it to their financial farms.

I asked them a hard question: "What condition would your agricultural farms be in if you had operated them the way you operated your financial farms?"

After a moment of silence, one of them answered, "That kind of procedure would have put me out of the farming business long ago." One by one, each farmer agreed.

I am happy to report that before those meetings were over, each farmer repented of his lack of faith. They promised God they would never again violate this eighth law of the harvest in their finances. They promised that from then on they would sow *to* their financial harvests, no matter how their previous harvests had done.

A Hard Lesson to Learn

There is no way to calculate how many of God's children are at the bottom of the financial barrel because they violate this most important law. I am convinced the majority of Christians gauge the size of their offerings by their income, instead of by the size income they desire in the future.

Every church I have ever pastored was full of people who allowed their giving to be influenced by adverse economic circumstances. If there were rumors of factories closing, or any other pending financial crisis, the weekly offerings would immediately go down.

I remember specifically the days of a terrible gasoline crisis. The price of gasoline literally skyrocketed. As soon as this happened, the weekly income of the church dropped. I remember how earnestly I preached to my people that they were the sons of God. He would supply their needs if they would only rebuke fear and continue to give. During this crisis, no matter how hard I preached, church income stayed down. Finally, we had to lay off several needed staff members.

The financial backlash to our church was devastating. Jobs were lost; bankruptcies were filed; many people's special plans had to be rescheduled or even canceled. The plan of God for our congregation had to be postponed because of the lack of faith. I am convinced that if our church members had increased their giving during that time, their incomes would have increased. Neither they nor the church would have suffered the pains of insufficiency that we all experienced.

The Fear of Insufficiency

For some reason, the fear of insufficiency tends to overshadow our faith in God. In the book of I Kings, a woman almost brought about her own financial collapse because of this fear. Her barrel of meal was nearly empty, so she stopped giving to God. This almost caused her death and the death of her son. Through the fear of insufficiency, this godly woman decided to disobey the Lord's command to feed Elijah. This is how the Bible describes the event:

> **Arise, get thee to Zarephath, which belongeth to Zidon, and dwell there: behold, *I have commanded a widow woman there to sustain thee.***
> **I Kings 17:9**

This woman was under divine command to feed the prophet.

> **And she said . . . I have not a cake, but an handful of meal in a barrel, and a little oil in a cruse: and, behold, I am gathering two sticks, that I may go in and dress it for me and my son, that we may eat it, and die.**
> **I Kings 17:12**

This woman's rebellion was great. She was sinning with knowledge. God had commanded her to feed Elijah, but the fear of insufficiency had gripped her. It had brought her to the point of deciding not to obey her God.

> ... Elijah said unto her, *Fear not*; go and do as thou hast said: but make me thereof a little cake first, and bring it unto me, and after make for thee and for thy son.
>
> I Kings 17:13

Elijah attacked the problem, the *fear of insufficiency*. He encouraged her to give according to her future, bountiful harvest, not from her past shortage.

> For thus saith the Lord God of Israel, The barrel of meal shall not waste, neither shall the cruse of oil fail .... .
>
> I Kings 17:14

From her failing crop of meal and oil, she gave. Her victory came swiftly. The seed she planted began a miracle harvest for herself, her son, and Elijah.

> ... she went and did according to the saying of Elijah: and she, and he, and her house, did eat many days. And the barrel of meal wasted not, neither did the cruse of oil fail, according to the word of the Lord, which he spake by Elijah.
>
> I Kings 17:15, 16

A New Testament Widow Gives To Meet Her "Wants"

This same principle of giving toward a future harvest was followed by a widow in the New Testament. She sowed to a new, bigger harvest that would not only meet her *needs,* but would also bring her the things she *wanted.*

> . . . Jesus sat over against the treasury, and
> beheld how the people cast money into the treasury:
> and many that were rich cast in much.
>
> And there came a certain poor widow, and she
> threw in two mites, which make a farthing.
>
> And he called unto him his disciples, and saith
> unto them, Verily I say unto you, That this poor
> widow hath cast more in, than all they which have
> cast into the treasury:
>
> For all they did cast in of their abundance; but
> she *of her want* did cast in all that she had, even all
> her living.
>
> Mark 12:41-44

Look carefully, and you will see that this widow woman
wanted something. She did not give her two mites because
she didn't have enough to live on, but because she wanted
more than the bare necessities of life. She was greatly
hindered by the insufficiency of her previous harvests.

The *King James* translation says she literally *threw* her
offering into the treasury. With this gesture, she planted more
seed than she had ever planted before — *all* her living. This
action immediately caught the attention of Christ.

Big Sowing in the Midst of Famine

I would like to give one more illustration of this eighth
law from God's Word.

> . . . Isaac sowed in that land, and received in the
> same year an hundredfold: and the Lord blessed
> him.
>
> Genesis 26:12

Please take the time to read this whole account found in Genesis 26. Isaac was facing great need. Famine had gripped the Promised Land. Harvest after harvest had failed. He was overtaken by the fear of insufficiency.

Isaac made plans to leave the Promised Land, the land of God's provision. He was heading to Egypt, the land of man's provision. He came dangerously close to blocking God's ability to supply for his needs. Just in time, Isaac heard God's voice.

> . . . Go not down into Egypt . . . Sojourn in this land, and I will be with thee, and will bless thee . . . .
>
> Genesis 26:2, 3

Isaac was obedient. In the next few verses, you will find that he sowed precious seed into the famine-parched land. How foolish he must have seemed to the unbelievers. I can hear the inhabitants of the land chiding him, saying, "You fool! Don't you realize this is famine time? Nothing can grow. It is a waste of good seed to plant now. At a time like this, you should eat or sell or do something more reasonable with your seed."

Isaac used his faith as a shield against bad news and the advice of the best minds of his day. He boldly obeyed God. He knew that if no seed was sown, there was no hope for a harvest. He also knew that if he sowed only a little, he would reap only a small crop. To reap the large harvest he needed, he would have to sow much. (II Cor. 9:6.) By his act of faith in God, and in this eighth law of the harvest, Isaac became so rich that even the heathen Philistines envied him.

> ... the man (Isaac) **waxed great, and went for-**
> **ward, and grew until he became very great:**
> **For he had possession of flocks, and possession**
> **of herds, and great store of servants: and the Philis-**
> **tines envied him.**
> **Genesis 26:13, 14**

A Mexican Apple Farmer Got It Right

Several years ago I was speaking in a school of ministry in Monterrey, Mexico. Mexican nationals were in attendance from all parts of the country. I was ministering the message of the financial harvest. I was specifically teaching these people not to allow their circumstances to affect their offerings to God.

I was not aware of a certain apple farmer from the city of Saltillo who sat quietly in the midst of the audience. Although many people spoke to me after each session, this farmer and I never met personally during that meeting.

Recently, I met this farmer in a school of ministry in Torreon, Mexico. He asked for a special moment with me when it would be convenient. He wanted to tell me of a miracle that had taken place in his finances. This is the story he related to me.

He had given a substantial financial gift to our ministry during that meeting in Monterrey. He had given the money as a seed for a very great harvest of apples. He desperately needed this because he had experienced several flawed harvests in previous years. This had brought him to the brink of bankruptcy.

After giving his greatest financial gift ever, he returned home to Saltillo only to be met with the worst of news. An unexpected freeze had come the same night he had given his large offering. It had killed all the apple blossoms in every orchard in his area.

At this news, doubt almost overtook him. The fear of insufficiency was trying to make him accuse God of not honoring the seed he had sown. But he wisely said to his wife, "Let's pray, for we have faithfully sown to this harvest. We see the result of nature, and it doesn't look good, but we have a relationship with the God who rules over nature."

He and his wife prayed earnestly. With their prayers, they pushed back fear. The next fifteen days were agony to them as reports came in from across the valley. Everyone was saying, "No apple crop this year." Over and over again, these faithful servants of God had to bear the laughter and ridicule of their fellow farmers. In spite of this, they boldly continued to confess, "We will have an apple harvest. God will not fail us. We have sown in faith. By faith we will reap."

On the fifteenth day their miracle was manifested. On every tree where there had been a frozen blossom, a tiny apple had now begun to grow. At first they were only the size of pinheads, but they were alive and well. Each day they grew until they were fully ripe and ready to pick. This godly farmer had the only apple harvest in his valley that year. It was the most abundant harvest he had ever experienced.

Now get ready for the best part. Because of the total failure of every other apple crop in the valley, he received more per bushel for his apples than had ever been paid in that area before. This man and his wife are living testimonies to the truth of the eighth law of the harvest. We must sow *to* our future harvest size, not according to the insufficiency of a past harvest.

Sow Abundantly Toward a Greater Harvest

The very fact that you need a greater financial harvest witnesses to the insufficiency of your past harvest. Under these circumstances, be ever so careful when you sow. Your natural tendency will be to give offerings according to your financial shortage. Doing this will not solve your problem; it will only prolong and intensify its effect. It will cause you to experience yet other insufficient harvests.

Stop that old kind of thinking. Do not plant according to past insufficiency, but plant boldly toward future abundance. You might wonder how you can do this, seeing that you have so little. Do not forget what we have already learned in Chapter Five about faith-promise giving. Make a promise to give a certain amount; give what you can now, and pay the rest in payments.

With a faith promise, you are only obligated to give if God supplies you with what you pledged. If God fails to supply, you owe nothing. But remember, *God never fails*. If you make your promise in faith, nothing wavering, the balance of your promise will come.

It's Your Move

Determine today if your past harvests have been sufficient. If they have, continue to sow in the same way as always. If your past harvests have been less than enough, you must plant more than ever before. When you give more, you will reap more.

> **. . . if he plants much, he will reap much.**
> **II Corinthians 9:6 *TLB***

As our list of the laws of the harvest grows, there is a supernatural power growing in you and building your confidence.

Law #1: Your seed must be planted.

Law #2: You must render your seed useless.

Law #3: You must plant what you expect to harvest.

Law #4: Your harvest size is established when your seed is sown.

Law #5: Your seed must be planted in good ground.

Law #6: You must always wait a period of time between planting and harvesting.

Law #7: You must maintain your crops for a proper harvest.

Law #8: You must always sow to your harvest size, not from your harvest size.

10

The Ninth Law of the Harvest:
Your Expense Is Always Highest at Harvest Time

> ... the kingdom of heaven is like unto a man
> that is an householder, which went out early in the
> morning to hire labourers into his vineyard.
> **Matthew 20:1**

As a group of college students ate their lunch in a small diner, their conversation was overheard by a middle-aged busboy. The students were loudly complaining about the high cost of their educations. The busboy listened intently to the bellyaching of the students. When he could hold back no longer, he said, "If you think education is expensive, you should try ignorance, as I have!"

I doubt that any of those students ever heard more truth in fewer words.

Ignorance of God's laws of the harvest has been responsible for the cancellation of more financial harvests than any other single factor. Strange as it may seem, the ninth law is virtually unknown to the Christian church. Again and again, I hear Christians say, "I gave big a few years ago, and now, after patiently waiting, almost nothing has happened. A few dollars have come in, but I know in my heart it is not the harvest God intended."

By now you have learned there are many painstaking steps the farmer must take before he can experience a harvest.

117

He must plant his seed. He must plant in the good ground. He must care for his crops as they grow. As costly as all these steps may be, they are not the most expensive steps he will have to take.

The Day of Greatest Expense

On the day the crop is ripe, the farmer must hire laborers to break the harvest loose from the stalk. A substantial cost is always incurred by the farmer just before he is able to realize the full benefit of his harvest.

I cannot over-emphasize the importance of this law of the harvest. If only someone had written a book like this one when my wife and I were first pioneering the financial harvest. We would not have made so many mistakes. Yes, we made mistakes — plenty of them. Thank God, we finally got it right. This law of the harvest works for the farmer. It works for me; so it has to work for you, too!

. . . God is no respecter of persons.
Acts 10:34

With each increase of knowledge in the laws of the harvest, our harvest improved. Even as our knowledge grew, we were not experiencing the total abundance so clearly spoken of in God's Word. We knew there was more. We knew God would show it to us if we diligently sought for answers. What I am about to share with you was discovered quite by accident. As we stumbled into it, we had no idea we were being shown one of the most important laws of the harvest. Since learning this principle, we regularly experience abundant harvests.

The Key to Abundant Harvest

God spoke to us a few years ago to give a large financial gift of $42,000.00 to Trinity Broadcasting Network. It took tremendous faith on our part. We did not have the money, so we made a faith promise to pay it within six months. Without going into detail, let me say God performed a financial miracle. We received two exceptional financial gifts. The entire $42,000.00 was paid two weeks before the six months expired. Praise the Lord!

After this, we continued to give offerings. A year passed without any sign of a harvest. We knew God was faithful, but we also knew something was not operating properly. We had sown big. We had sown in faith. Now we sensed our harvest was ripe, but nothing was happening. We felt helpless. What could we do? It was as if our hands were tied.

Many of God's people know exactly what I am talking about. When your harvest is ripe, there is an unction that tells you, *"It is time for harvest."*

About this same time, I priced a new car. I have always enjoyed cars, and I really wanted to trade for a new model. I was somewhat disappointed to learn it would cost $12,000.00, plus my old car, to make the trade.

The old car was far from worn out, but I just got the "new car bug." I get unreasonable when this bug bites. My wife, bless her heart, has the unpleasant task of seeing me through these times of weakness.

That evening, my wife and I traveled to Dallas, Texas,

to be part of a special Trinity Broadcasting Network camp meeting. The conversation of purchasing a new car was temporarily overshadowed by our anticipation of seeing Paul, Jan, and the TBN family. As we rode down the highway, my wife suddenly said, "John, let's not spend our $12,000.00 on a new car. Instead, let's give it to Paul Crouch tonight to help pay for the new Dallas/Ft. Worth studio TBN is building."

It took me only a moment to reply, "Yes, let's do it." I was in total agreement with her. I would much rather give the money to a ministry than to an automaker.

Upon our arrival at the camp meeting, we told Paul we would be giving him $12,000.00 toward the construction of the new station. We also put some works with our faith. We handed him a check for $1,000.00, promising to send the other $11,000.00 as soon as we could.

The Flood Gates Open

Well, let me tell you, almost instantly the flood gates of our abundant harvest broke open. Money seemed to come to us from everywhere. In less than a year, every bill our ministry owed was paid. Four of the ministry's parsonages were paid off. Why, in just short of a year, $250,000.00 came from everywhere. *I mean everywhere.* We were totally debt free.

Now hold on. That's not all. Keep this $250,000.00 in mind. There is still more to tell. His Image Ministries, the ministry God has given my wife and me to work through, had been operating for several years with offices in our home. It had grown until it took over almost every room in our house.

As we outgrew the house, in desperation, we rented a small office. The suite adjacent to our office was vacant and under long-term lease to a person who did not need the space. He assured me that he had no intention of using it, and it would be available to us when we needed it.

Within a very short time, our ministry expanded to double its previous size; then it doubled again. Once again we were totally out of space. I went to the man next door and told him I now needed to rent the extra space. He said, "I have bad news for you. Next week I am moving a business into that space. It is no longer available."

Now what was I going to do? Would I be forced to move supplemental offices back into my house? I can remember our prayer, "Lord, please, not that!"

To fully understand the extent of this story, I must tell you something else that was happening during this time. For three years I had been keeping my eye on a beautiful, new office building just a few blocks from my house. It was very spacious, and I felt it was perfect for us. The only problem was that it cost $550,000.00, much more than I felt comfortable with paying.

During the past few months, several changes had occurred. The builder of the office complex had gone into bankruptcy. This had lowered the price to $400,000.00. It was an improvement, but it was still far too much money to spend for an office.

I should not be amazed at how quickly God changes circumstances for His children, but I always am. On the same day I found I would not be able to rent the much -needed office space next door, I also learned the bank that repossessed this beautiful new office had now come to the brink of bankruptcy. They were receiving any and all offers on the building. With this news, I wrote a proposal to purchase it for $300,000.00.

Within a few days our offer was accepted, and we were moving in. Remember, the initial sales price was $550,000.00. On the day we bought the building, we paid only $300,000.00. We had saved $250,000.00 off the original sales price. Add it up. $250,000.00 worth of debts and mortgages paid off, plus the $250,000.00 direct savings on our new office building. Why, God had given us $500,000.00 (one half million) in just short of two years after planting our $42,000.00 seed in the good ground.

A Special Offering Released Our Harvest

Yes, we also gave offerings all along the way, *but it wasn't until we gave the $12,000.00 offering that the abundant harvest was released.* It was at this time we realized we had found a key law of the harvest that would release our harvests again and again when they became ripe.

The farmer faces his greatest additional expense when he has to hire reapers to gather the harvest. In the same way, we also must make a substantial expenditure by giving a special *harvest release offering* just as we sense our financial harvest is fully ripe and ready to be reaped.

> **. . . the kingdom of heaven is like unto a man
> that is an householder, which went out early in the
> morning to *hire labourers* into his vineyard.**
> **Matthew 20:1**

Please realize that you need spiritual discernment to know when your financial fields are white unto harvest.

Is Your Financial Harvest Ready?

Many of God's children are due abundant harvests, but they do not receive them because of their ignorance of this ninth law. Ask God if this special *harvest-release offering* is not the key you have been looking for. Put this principle to work in your life right now. Write a substantial check, and send it to one of the good-ground ministries.

The sooner this law of the harvest is put into action, the sooner your overdue harvest will be released. Add this special truth to your steadily growing list.

Law #1: Your seed must be planted.

Law #2: You must render your seed useless.

Law #3: You must plant what you expect to harvest.

Law #4: Your harvest size is established when your seed is sown.

Law #5: Your seed must be planted in good ground.

Law #6: You must always wait a period of time between planting and harvesting.

Law #7: You must maintain your crops for a a proper harvest.

Law #8: You must always sow to your harvest size, not from your harvest size.

Law #9: Your expense is always highest at harvest time.

11

The Tenth Law of the Harvest:
A Part of Your Harvest Is for Sowing Again

> ... God, who gives seed to the farmer to plant, and later on, good crops to harvest and eat, *will give you more and more seed to plant* and will make it grow so that you can give away more and more fruit from your harvest.
>
> **II Corinthians 9:10 *TLB***

What do you call a farmer who eats all of his harvest? A fool! Surely you cannot call him a farmer any longer, for every true farmer always saves some seed from each harvest for replanting.

The Foolishness of the One-Time Harvest

Several years ago, while pastoring in Southern California, I delivered a strong series of sermons to my congregation on sowing and reaping finances. I concluded the series with a strong appeal to put God to the test by planting a substantial financial seed into the ministry. I encouraged them to believe God for an increase, and then report back to me with the results.

I was amazed at how quickly almost everyone received a great financial harvest. As you can imagine, the church was astir with testimonies. I felt good that the people had not only learned the Word of God, but they had experienced a positive result from putting it into action.

After a period of several months, I began to ask the people individually how they were progressing with subsequent sowing and reaping. To my utter amazement, I found that only about one out of ten of them ever replanted any of the money from their harvests. They had foolishly spent it all on themselves. The more people I spoke to, the more disappointed I became. Not only did they fail to replant, but over 60% of them had not even tithed on their original harvest.

Forgetting What We Look Like

How strange a creature the Christian can be. No wonder the book of James describes us as those who see ourselves in a mirror, and then immediately forget what we look like.

> ... he is like unto a man beholding his natural face in a glass:
>
> For he beholdeth himself, and goeth his way, and straightway forgetteth what manner of man he was.
>
> **James 1:23, 24**

The saints of God see what they are to be like each time they read the Bible (mirror). It describes us as possessing faith, integrity, healing power, and dominion over Satan. The mystery is that immediately after reading what the Bible says, we forget who it says we are in Christ. We then foolishly return to being who we were before we were saved.

Often when we experience a financial harvest, we rejoice, knowing the increase is from God. We know it is our right to have abundance, for we are the children of God. Then we foolishly lavish it all upon ourselves, never replanting any of it back into a good-ground ministry.

We have forgotten who we are. We are the ones God promised would have the "power to get wealth" in order to fund His covenant. (Deut. 8:18.)

Look at God's Word. He is more than willing to give you an abundant harvest. He sincerely desires to meet your every need. However, He expects you to replant a portion. A part of every harvest is to be used to give generously toward spreading the good news that Jesus died for the sins of the world.

> ... God, who gives seed to the farmer to plant, and later on, good crops to harvest and eat, *will give you more and more seed to plant* and will make it grow so that you can give away more and more fruit from your harvest.
> Yes, God will give you much so that you can give away much .... .
>
> **II Corinthians 9:10, 11 *TLB***

Be a Farmer, Not a Fool

Do not let the adverse circumstances of your everyday life block you from experiencing your next harvest. After you have put the principle of sowing and reaping finances to work, have the good sense to direct a portion of every harvest back into the gospel ministry.

If you make a practice of faithfully doing this, *I praise God* for your wisdom and faith. If you have foolishly eaten all your seed, don't despair! You have not eternally blown it! Remember, the laws of the harvest are perpetual. They are always in operation. You can plant again any time.

> **While the earth remaineth, seedtime and harvest . . . shall not cease.**
> **Genesis 8:22**

Just begin right now with a generous gift into a good-ground ministry. It will soon come up and bring forth a harvest for you. The important thing is to act now, for each day you wait is another day's delay before reaping your harvest.

Jesus' Lifestyle Was Giving

Jesus lived a lifestyle of giving! He clearly declared this when He said:

> **. . . I am come that they might have life, and that they might have it *more abundantly*.**
> **John 10:10**

His habitual giving was evidenced by the reaction of His disciples when He dismissed Judas from the table of the "last supper." They were so accustomed to His lifestyle of giving, they immediately supposed he was sending Judas to give money to the poor.

> **. . . some of them thought, because Judas had the bag, that Jesus had said unto him . . . that he should give something to the poor.**
> **John 13:29**

We are told in the Word of God we should be changing from glory unto glory into His marvelous image. How wonderful it will be when all the Church comes into this grace. Instead of hearing how Christians are meager givers, people will say our lifestyle is giving. I like the sound of that!

Giving Does Not Seem To Come Naturally

Throughout the gospels, Jesus encouraged His disciples to give. Despite this, they stubbornly continued to display the characteristics of their old natures. When the woman with the alabaster box came to anoint Jesus, as soon as she began to lavish her rich gift upon Him, she was sternly rebuked by those closest to Him.

> ... when His disciples saw it, they had indigna-
> tion, saying, To what purpose is this waste?
> **Matthew 26:8**

Giving to God is not a waste! It is a guaranteed way of multiplying that which is given.

> **Give, and it shall be given unto you; good
> measure, pressed down, and shaken together, and
> running over, shall men give into your bosom. For
> with the same measure that ye mete withal it shall be
> measured to you again.**
> **Luke 6:38**

How strange it is that the children of God consistently miss this most obvious promise when it comes to giving. In my personal experience I have seen the ugliest side of Christians when it came to giving to God. The worst is not seen when they fall to the depths of what man calls "gross" sin. The ugliest side comes forth when they fall to the depths of greed. No manifestation of human nature is less godlike than greed and selfishness.

Fools Eat the Seed Corn

Let me illustrate with the following story the folly of eating that which we should plant. A colony was being established by a band of settlers on a remote island located far from the normal shipping lanes. Settlers were left there with an agreement that a ship would return to check on their progress in about five years. The colonists were well equipped with sufficient provisions for a year, and enough seed to provide an abundant harvest for the future.

As they began to prepare the ground for farming, a most wonderful thing happened. Just below the surface of the ground they found many large gemstones. Everywhere they plowed, up came hundreds of precious stones. Needless to say, they declared their venture to be an instant success. Millions of dollars in gems were quickly amassed.

During this first year, only a few seeds were sown. There seemed to be little time for farming as everyone was so busy becoming a millionaire. Every inhabitant of the new colony became rich beyond his wildest dreams.

At the end of the year, only a small corn harvest was gathered because so little had been planted. During the second year, even greater discoveries of gemstones were made. All of the first harvest was eaten, but none was replanted. Everyone was just too busy mining gemstones to plant corn seed.

The end of the third year found them in a hopeless situation. Everyone was fabulously wealthy, but no one had anything to eat. Now they were face to face with their folly, for it would be two full years before the next ship would arrive.

Need I go further? This island full of millionaires became an island full of failures because they neglected a basic law of the harvest. Part of every harvest is for sowing again.

When the ship arrived at the end of five years, all that remained of the settlers were their dead bodies. Yes, these people had riches untold, but rich or poor, only a fool eats the seed corn.

So many Christians foolishly exchange a one-time blessing for the perpetual blessing of the harvest by not replanting some of the seed (money).

Thousands of Gallons of Water in a Pint Bottle

Many years ago, in the great Mohave Desert of America, there was a small oasis. It was located midway across the most treacherous portion of the desert. At this strategic point, every traveler needed water.

In the middle of this oasis was a well with an old-fashioned hand pump. To make the pump operate, its handle had to be vigorously moved up and down until a stream of clear water would pour forth. Everyone who passed that way spoke of the importance of the well. It was considered man's best friend in that part of the world.

One day, as a group of travelers was seated around the well enjoying the benefits of its cool, clear water, they began to reflect on its great importance. The guide who led them there listened intently as each spoke words of admiration for the well and its precious life-giving flow of water. After a while, he said, "The well and the pump are not the most important things at this oasis!"

With this statement, the weary travelers began to look around for some great treasure they might have overlooked in their hurry to drink of the well's stream. After a careful examination of the bleak terrain, one of the travelers spoke. "I beg to disagree. I see nothing that can even begin to approach the importance of this well!"

The guide replied, "Look at the little pint bottle of water hanging from the well. That little, old bottle, with its tight cork, holds the most important thing at this site. It contains the water needed for priming the pump. Before the well can give up its precious water, you must pour the contents of that bottle into the well shaft to wet the leather seals at the bottom. That water moistens and expands the leather so a vacuum can be produced in the pump to bring up water from the bottom of the well.

"Many travelers have been found dead here because they did not have the faith to pour that pint of water down the well shaft. They drank it instead and then perished from thirst because they did not obey the law that operates the pump. You have to give it a drink of water before it can deliver a stream of water."

Your seed is God's promise to you of a future harvest. If you eat it, it will deliver only a short-term benefit. However, if you exercise your God-given faith and plant it, it will *prime the pump of God's abundance and bring forth a refreshing harvest.*

The Planted Seed Is More Powerful Than the Eaten Seed

Do not get confused on this point. The most important part of every harvest is not the part you eat, but it is the part you faithfully plant again. The miracle of the perpetual financial harvest depends upon your ability to plant a portion of your finances back into the Gospel. If this law of the harvest is faithfully performed, you will not just receive a one-time blessing, but you will receive an unending succession of harvests that will meet your every need and desire.

I Cannot Emphasize It Enough

There is a vast difference between a one-time blessing and continuing success. Anyone who sows into the good ground can have a good harvest once, but only those who sow again and again will experience success from harvest to harvest. There is nothing to hinder this process from working throughout your entire life.

You can harvest over and over as long as you plant from each harvest. Yes! You can harvest until Jesus returns if you will not grow weary in well doing, and sow again from each new harvest.

> **...for whatsoever a man soweth, that shall he also reap.**
>
> **Galatians 6:7**

You only reap when you sow. The tenth law of the harvest must be observed if you choose to have successive harvests. Part of every harvest is for sowing again. Remember, God will give you more and more seed to plant. (II Cor. 9:10.)

Law #1:   Your seed must be planted.

Law #2:   You must render your seed useless.

Law #3:   You must plant what you expect to harvest.

Law #4:   Your harvest size is established when your seed is sown.

Law #5:   Your seed must be planted in good ground.

Law #6:   You must always wait a period of time between planting and harvesting.

Law #7:   You must maintain your crops for a proper harvest.

Law #8:   You must always sow to your harvest size, not from your harvest size.

Law #9:   Your expense is always highest at harvest time.

Law #10: A part of your harvest is for sowing again.

12

The Eleventh Law of the Harvest:
A Part of Your Harvest Is for You To Keep

> ... who planteth a vineyard, and eateth not of
> the fruit thereof?
>
> **I Corinthians 9:7**

There are those who teach that Christians are not to have any material possessions, or limited possessions at best. This idea has attracted followers throughout church history. Even today, the predominant mentality throughout the church is that God wants His children to be poor.

Many wonderful people adhere to this philosophy. It does not seem to cause them to love Jesus any less. They do, however, have a distorted definition of spirituality. They seem to believe God is especially pleased with anyone who has given up all of life's comforts for Him. In the extreme cases of this belief, they may even feel abundance is a sign of sin. This theology has left the Church at the edge of bankruptcy, and most church members barely able to survive. It is almost totally void of any balance or biblical basis.

Kingdom Stewardship

Other than the Bible, there is little information about Kingdom stewardship. Kingdom stewardship is the biblical teaching that we (God's children) are to have *all sufficiency,* actually more than enough to meet all our needs and desires.

135

But it doesn't stop there. It goes on to teach that we will have an abundant surplus to give generously into every endeavor where God directs.

> ... cheerful givers are the ones God prizes.
> II Corinthians 9:7 *TLB*

It is clear from the Scriptures God does not want His children pressured into giving more than they want. He wants our giving to be voluntary and joyful. He says He especially enjoys our giving when it is done cheerfully. It is difficult to be a cheerful giver when you constantly walk in insufficiency.

> God is able to make it up to you by giving you everything you need and more, so that there will not only be enough for your own needs, but *plenty* left over to give joyfully to others.
> II Corinthians 9:8 *TLB*

Please keep in mind, these words are not the words of a man, but the words of our God. God says He is able to make up to you everything you have given. This is not a promise to return to you only as much as you have given. It is a promise to multiply it back to you in such abundance that it will meet your every need and desire. It is clear. The person who gives finances to God is entitled to have enough returned to him for his own use.

In addition, there will be a surplus that goes beyond his own needs and wants. This surplus is not spoken of as being only a small amount, but it is described as *plenty*.

> ... not only enough for your own needs, but plenty left over ....
> II Corinthians 9:8 *TLB*

The Harvest Belongs to the Sower

The seed (money) planted was yours, so the harvest (money) reaped is *also* yours.

> . . . so that you can give away more and more fruit from *your* harvest.
>
> **II Corinthians 9:10** *TLB*

It is not the Lord's harvest. It is not the ground's harvest. It belongs to you, the one who planted. The Bible shows who owns the harvest and abounds with proof of the owner's right to eat of it.

> . . . who planteth a vineyard, and eateth not of the fruit thereof? or who feedeth a flock, and eateth not of the milk of the flock . . . .
> Thou shalt not muzzle the mouth of the ox that treadeth out the corn . . . .
> this is written: that he that ploweth should plow in hope; and that he that thresheth in hope should be partaker of his hope.
>
> **I Corinthians 9:7, 9, 10**

> Whoso keepeth the fig tree shall eat the fruit thereof . . . .
>
> **Proverbs 27:18**

> . . . every man should eat and drink, and enjoy the good of all his labour, it is the gift of God.
>
> **Ecclesiastes 3:13**

> There is nothing better for a man, than that he should eat and drink, and that he should make his soul enjoy good in his labor. . . .
>
> **Ecclesiastes 2:24**

> ... trust ... in the living God, who giveth us
> richly all things to enjoy.
>
> I Timothy 6:17

Throughout the Bible, God invites us to eat our fill from the abundance of every harvest He brings forth from our seed. Please do not draw back from enjoying your portion of your harvest because of the misunderstanding of others. God desires you to live the good life. He wants you to have proper housing, warm clothing, nutritious food, dependable transportation, relaxing vacations, profitable investments, and a comfortable retirement.

None of these are bad things if they are kept in their proper perspective. Remember the words of Jesus.

> ... take no thought, saying, What shall we eat? or, What shall we drink? or, Wherewithal shall we be clothed?
> (For after all these things do the Gentiles seek:) for your heavenly Father knoweth that *ye have need of all these things.*
> But *seek ye first* the kingdom of God, and His righteousness; and all these things shall be added unto you.
>
> Matthew 6:31-33

God knows you need things. There is nothing wrong with having your needs and desires adequately provided.

We Have Been Taught To Be Poor

Several years ago, I was about to address a church just outside Capetown in South Africa. Prior to my lesson on abundance, the congregation was being led in the song, "He Is All I Need." They sang it through for about ten minutes, then introduced me.

I opened my message by saying the song was beautifully done, but it contradicted the teaching of Jesus. Well, you can imagine the stir that followed. I then opened my Bible and read Matthew 6:32, ... **your heavenly Father knoweth that ye have *need* of all of these things.**

These poor folks had been without the bare necessities of life for so long, they fed on that song as if it were a narcotic. They sang it over and over again, "He is all I need, all I need. Jesus is all I need." It somehow seemed to dull the pain of their insufficiency. Traditional teachings had locked this whole segment of the Capetown society into poverty and want.

Do not let tradition intimidate you. God does not mind if you keep a part of your harvest to eat and enjoy. He knows you need *all these things*.

You Are Worthy of Your God-Given Reward

It was Jesus who made the statement, "the workman is worthy of his meat." This truth is repeated throughout the New Testament. (Matt. 10:10; Luke 10:7; I Tim. 5:18.)

If you give in accordance with the laws of the harvest and live a life consistent with God's Word, you will reap a harvest. When this harvest is reaped, a substantial portion of it will be for the express purpose of your enjoyment.

139

Some Christians Do Not Want You To Enjoy Your Increase

During the last few years, I have given away a dozen or more watches. Each time I gave one away, more watches were given to me. Eventually, I received a genuine gold watch which I gave to Evangelist LaVerne Tripp. Almost immediately, I received another gold watch. I gave it to Pastor Bennie Hinn. Then I received one of the finest gold watches made in the world. If I mentioned the brand name, almost everyone would recognize it.

I have also given away many rings. After doing this several times, I received a very special ring I really liked. No sooner had I received it than a special pastor friend, Stephen Munsey, mentioned how attractive it was. Immediately the Lord impressed me to give it to him. I really didn't want to, so I knew it was not my idea to give it away. I knew it was God instructing me.

Not long after giving it to him, I was given another ring more valuable and more beautiful than any I had ever dreamed of owning. It was a direct gift from God to me. It was my harvest from all the rings I had planted.

Now you might think this is a wonderful thing. Let me tell you the problem I have faced since receiving these wonderful blessings from God. Some of my Christian brothers are very unhappy with me when they see me wearing this beautiful watch and ring. They think I should sell them or give them away. Anything I might do with them would be acceptable — except wearing them. Some say it is sending the wrong signal to those who do not have enough. Some say it is a sign of worldliness to wear good gold jewelry.

What am I to do? Hide them? Wear them only when I am away from those less fortunate than me? How can I do that when Jesus said I will have the poor with me always? (Matt. 26:11.)

And how about Jesus? Should He have rebuked the woman with the alabaster box of expensive ointment? Does He intend us to hide our blessing? I took this problem to God. I told Him I would gladly sell my jewelry or give it away, but He impressed me not to do that. He said, "You have sown watches and rings, and this very good watch and this precious ring are the result of a biblical principle you have followed. They are evidence of the accuracy and dependability of my Word. They are to be worn. They are a part of your harvest that is yours to keep and enjoy without feeling guilty."

The church must learn that a portion of every harvest is for the sower to keep and enjoy. *The gifts of God are from Him to us.*

We cannot allow the misconception of others to dictate what we eat, where we live, what we drive, what we wear. If everyone walks at the level of those who have the least faith, the least understanding of God's abundant supply, soon we will all walk in poverty.

We Are To Please God, Not Men

Imagine how displeasing it would be to you if you gave your children beautiful, new coats, only to find they would not

141

wear them because none of their friends had received new coats from their parents.

God is your Father. If you, His beautiful child, properly sow your finances and live a life pleasing to Him, you are going to experience a financial harvest. When this happens you must sow a generous portion of it back into the Gospel, but that which remains is for you and your family to enjoy. It is the fruit of your labor. It is lovingly given to you by your Heavenly Father to meet your needs and desires. The last thing God wants you to feel when He blesses you is guilt. He is the One who has given you the abundant increase. Guilt feelings find their origin in the person of Satan. Rest assured, feelings of guilt do not come from God.

Jesus Had a Nice Home

Many of the misinformed teach us we should be poor because Jesus was poor. They say He did not even have a home to live in, and they sanctimoniously quote:

> **. . . foxes have holes, and the birds of the air have nests; but the Son of man hath not where to lay his head.**
> **Matthew 8:20**

Before you fall for this partial truth, read the whole passage. You will quickly see *why* Jesus had no place to lay His head that night. He had planned to stay with the Samaritans. His lead team arrived well ahead of Him to prepare a place. The Samaritans refused to give Him lodging because of their religious differences with the Jews.

Contrary to the teachings of men, the Bible shows that Jesus did have a home.

> ... Jesus turned, and saw them following, and saith unto them, What seek ye? They said unto Him, Rabbi ... where dwellest thou?
>
> He saith unto them, *come and see.* They came and saw where He dwelt, and abode with Him that day.... .
>
> John 1:38, 39

Jesus Had Nice Clothes

Scripture also teaches that Jesus had nice clothing. He did not walk about in drab, non-stylish attire. This is adequately documented in John's gospel.

> ... the soldiers, when they had crucified Jesus, took His garments, and made four parts, to every soldier a part; and also His coat:*now the coat was without seam, woven from the top throughout.*
>
> They said therefore among themselves, Let us not rend it, but cast lots for it, whose it shall be ... .
>
> John 19:23, 24

The coat Jesus wore was of such a high quality, the soldiers dared not tear it. If it were described in today's language, it would have been called a *designer coat.* The value was so great, they cast lots for it.

Do not let the old, non-scriptural arguments about Jesus living in poverty confuse you. He had *everything* He needed and more.

No Guilt Trips Allowed

. . . if you give little, you will get little . . . .
II Corinthians 9:6 *TLB*

The church has no trouble accepting this portion of the verse. We gladly concede it is all right to teach anything that will cause the saints of God to get little. I have never been maligned by anyone for speaking of shortage and hard times for Christians. However, the verse does not stop with the promise of getting little. Read on and see a better way of planting.

. . . but if he plants much, he will reap much.
II Corinthians 9:6 *TLB*

You see, the choice is yours. Your harvest is controlled by your giving, and God does not put any pressure on the giver.

. . . Don't force anyone to give more than he really wants to, for cheerful givers are the ones God prizes.
II Corinthians 9:7 *TLB*

If you want little, just sow little. God doesn't mind! It is up to you. Just don't be deceived into expecting a big harvest from only a few seeds.

If you desire a big harvest, then you must plant abundantly. If you sow much, the Word says you will reap much. It is your choice.

I encourage you to cast down all the evil imaginations that make you feel guilty about enjoying your rightful portion. Go ahead and enjoy all the good things. They are your reward for being a faithful steward. You are the one who has sown liberally into the work of God. According to Scripture, you are entitled to reap a generous harvest from God — a harvest that is *yours* to enjoy without guilt. My advice is to plant much, so you can reap much.

Law #1:   Your seed must be planted.

Law #2:   You must render your seed useless.

Law #3:   You must plant what you expect to harvest.

Law #4:   Your harvest size is established when your seed is sown.

Law #5:   Your seed must be planted in good ground.

Law #6:   You must always wait a period of time between planting and harvesting.

Law #7:   You must maintain your crops for a proper harvest.

Law #8:   You must always sow to your harvest size, not from your harvest size.

Law #9:   Your expense is always highest at harvest time.

Law #10:   A part of your harvest is for sowing again.

Law #11:   A part of your harvest is for you to keep.

13

The Twelfth Law of the Harvest:
Your Harvest Is a Miracle

I have planted, Apollos watered; but God gave the increase.
I Corinthians 3:6

No factory has ever manufactured a seed that can reproduce itself. No laboratory has ever made a seed that can multiply itself into a harvest.

Only God can make seed that multiplies. You will find this in the first book of the Bible. Seed is not manufactured. It is produced from other seed. Its origin is not in the genus of creation, but in the *power* of the Creator.

> **... God said, Let the earth bring forth grass, the herb yielding seed, and the fruit tree yielding fruit after his kind, whose seed is in itself, upon the earth: and it was so.**
> **And the earth brought forth grass, and herb yielding seed after his kind, and the tree yielding fruit, whose seed was in itself, after his kind: and God saw that it was good.**
> **Genesis 1:11, 12**

The above verses deal specifically with the origin and purpose of seed. God says within the grasses, trees, and herbs there is seed. Each seed is a miracle capsule that will perpetually reproduce the kind of vegetation it came from.

There Is a Miracle in Every Seed

The book of Mark speaks of the hidden miracle that lies inside every seed.

> . . . So is the kingdom of God, as if a man should cast seed into the ground;
> And should sleep, and rise night and day, and the seed should spring and grow up, *he knoweth not how*.
> For the earth bringeth forth fruit of herself; first the blade, then the ear, after that the full corn in the ear.
> But when the fruit is brought forth, immediately he putteth in the sickle, because the harvest is come.
>
> **Mark 4:26-29**

Notice the words, *"he knoweth not how."* Two thousand years have passed since this statement was made, yet the secret still stands today. Although modern man knows many things that can be done to increase the yield of seed, he still does not know how the seed becomes a harvest.

Certain seed can be cross-pollinated, and hybrids can be produced through this process. However, no matter what we do, no man, or process, or machine can make a seed. Every seed has to pass through a miracle stage before it can reproduce. The divine intervention of God is absolutely necessary each time.

It does not matter if an agricultural farmer believes in miracles. A miracle must take place before his seed can become a harvest. He must allow God to work. He cannot pry the harvest out of the seed. He cannot blast the harvest from inside the seed. He must just leave it alone, under the proper conditions, allowing God to work the miracle.

There Are Many Harvests

The Bible speaks of the multiplication of seed in several harvests. It speaks of this process occurring in the agricultural harvest. It speaks of the harvest of mankind at the end of the age. It speaks of the financial harvest.

God is involved in the return experienced in every harvest. He sees to it that a harvest is manifested according to what has been planted.

> **Be not deceived; God is not mocked: for whatsoever a man soweth, that shall he also reap.**
> **Galations 6:7**

Christians who desire to optimize their harvests must recognize that the Lord plays the major role in its manifestation.

Formulas and Mechanical Confessions

Always remember that when a harvest occurs, a miracle has taken place. Harvest always necessitates the intervention of God. There cannot be a harvest without Him. He is the giver of life.

There is a trend among Christians to reduce the operation of the harvest to a mechanical process or to a carefully rehearsed confession. You can plant a good seed in good ground. You can water and weed it. You can wait patiently for it to grow, but *unless God gives the increase,* nothing will happen.

> . . . God gave the increase.
> I Corinthians 3:6

A farmer can receive an agricultural harvest by following a mechanical formula. Seed of the botanical kingdom can be multiplied, even if it is planted by a lost man.

There is a higher realm of planting and reaping. In this realm there are special harvests. The Bible tells us of the multiplication of money, the multiplication of loaves and fishes, the multiplication of friends, and so on. When you enter this supernatural realm, you cannot multiply your seed by operating a formula. *There must be a relationship with God* in order to manifest these special harvests.

The spirit world is greatly affected by the heart of the person who is operating the laws of the harvest. Your financial harvest is a highly spiritual matter. The Lord's part in it will have to be acknowledged and diligently sought after.

Faith Moves God's Hand in the Harvest

Jesus instructs us to use His name when we desire anything from God, the Father. So it only makes sense that when you have planted financial seed, you should approach the Father, in the name of Jesus, and ask Him to optimize your harvest. Remember, Jesus said that God will do whatever we ask Him to do in His name.

> . . . whatsoever ye shall ask of the Father in my
> name, he may give it you.
> John 15:16

Faith in the name of Jesus Christ is the highest form of faith. All the spirit world, as well as all the physical world, must give way to the faith-filled child of God who speaks in the name of Jesus.

> ... even the devils are subject unto us through thy name.
>
> **Luke 10:17**

> ... God also hath highly exalted him, and given him a name which is above every name:
> That at the name of Jesus every knee should bow, of things in heaven, and things in earth, and things under the earth ... .
>
> **Philippians 2:9, 10**

Everything must come into submission to His name—not only in heaven and in earth, but everything *under* the earth as well. Keep in mind, seed germinates *under* the earth. Your seed can be stimulated to greater growth if you speak to it in the name of Jesus. Command your seed to come forth in a great harvest in His name.

Every time you give your financial seed (money), boldly pray to God in the name of Jesus for your seed to bring forth an abundant harvest. Speak to God often of the money you have planted. Pray fervently for the ministry to which you have given. Speak positive words of life to your seed. Keep the way clear of obstacles.

Mountains of Impossibility

Any number of mountains may stand between you and your harvest. There are economic situations such as unemployment, depression, recession, political upheavals. Your mountain may be the lack of job skills, opportunity, or even a lack of education. All of these may seem like great obstacles that block the possibility of a harvest.

You must realize these obstacles will not go away by themselves. You must have God intervene. He will help you move them if you properly use the name of Jesus. Every mountain of opposition you face, even the mountain of debt, must move when unwavering faith in His name is exercised.

> **. . . Jesus answering saith unto them, Have faith in God.** (Literally, Have the faith of God.)
> **For verily I say unto you, That whosoever** (that's you) **shall say unto this mountain** (whatever stands in the way of your harvest), *Be thou removed* **and be thou cast into the sea; and** *shall not doubt* **in his heart** (the God-kind of faith never doubts), **but shall believe that those things which he saith shall come to pass; he shall have whatsoever he saith.**
> **Therefore I say unto you, What things soever ye desire** (your harvest), **when ye pray, believe that ye receive them, and ye shall have them.**
> **Mark 11:22-24**

I cannot over-emphasize the need to ask for the blessings of God upon every seed you sow. God must always act first before your seed can multiply. Our Bible promises us God will act if we properly ask Him. Prayer is a necessary part of every financial harvest.

You Must Not Doubt

The following verse says when you exercise the God-kind of faith, it is important not to doubt.

. . . shall not doubt in his heart. . . .
Mark 11:23

You must shield your faith from doubt. When doubt is allowed to mix with your faith, it will weaken, then kill it. Strong faith is of the utmost importance to the multiplication of your harvest. There is a period of time when your entire harvest depends upon your faith for its existence.

Now faith is the *substance* of things hoped for, the evidence of things not seen.
Hebrews 11:1

The word *substance* used in this verse can be better understood if you substitute the words *raw material*. Your faith in God to multiply your money back to you is the raw material from which your harvest will be made.

When you allow doubt to enter your spirit, you are allowing the cancellation of your harvest. When your faith is gone, your harvest goes with it.

Your faith is also the evidence that your harvest exists in the spirit realm. Everything in the spirit realm is invisible. Everything that now exists visibly, existed first in the invisible (spirit) realm.

Through faith we understand that the worlds were framed by the word of God, so that *things which are seen were not made of things which do appear.*
Hebrews 11:3

Guard your heart against doubt, for it can cancel your financial harvest. Remember, faith is the doorway between the invisible and the visible realms. Your harvest will enter the visible through the door of your strong faith.

You Must Speak Right Words

Three times in this verse we are told the words we speak are critical to receiving what we ask for in faith.

> ... whosoever shall *say* unto this mountain, Be thou removed, and be thou cast into the sea; and shall not doubt in his heart, but shall believe that those things which he *saith* shall come to pass; he shall have whatsoever he *saith*.
>
> **Mark 11:23**

Speak only words of victory concerning your financial harvest. Never speak words of doubt, fear, or destruction. Always keep a firm belief that God can do what He has promised you. Speak only those things that confirm your harvest. Never speak words that will cancel your harvest.

> ... shall not doubt in his heart, but shall believe that those things which he saith shall come to pass; he shall have whatsoever he saith.
>
> **Mark 11:23**

You Must Pray

The Scripture says when you pray, the things you desire are manifested.

**... What things soever ye desire, when ye pray,
believe that ye receive them, and ye shall have them.
Mark 11:24**

If you are a serious investor in the Gospel of Jesus Christ, you cannot afford to overlook your time in prayer. It is crucial that you petition God for an abundant return on the seed you have planted. Your Heavenly Father has the ultimate authority over your harvest. You have been invited to speak freely to Him.

Keep all of the laws of the harvest. Go over them from time to time and be sure you are in compliance. This is necessary for your great harvest.

Law #1:   Your seed must be planted.

Law #2:   You must render your seed useless.

Law #3:   You must plant what you expect to harvest.

Law #4:   Your harvest size is established when your seed is sown.

Law #5:   Your seed must be planted in good ground.

Law #6:   You must always wait a period of time between planting and harvesting.

Law #7:   You must maintain your crops for a proper harvest.

Law #8:   You must always sow to your harvest size, not from your harvest size.

Law #9:   Your expense is always highest at harvest time.

Law #10:   A part of your harvest is for sowing again.

Law #11:   A part of your harvest is for you to keep.

Law #12:   Your harvest is a miracle.

14

You Must Now Plant Your Financial Seed to a Great Harvest

> For God ... will give *you* ... *seed to plant* and
> will make it grow ....
>
> **II Corinthians 9:10 *TLB***

For some reason, the time never seems right for giving. There is always some adverse circumstance to hinder you. It may be that it is tax time. It may be pending lay-offs in your industry. Your car may need unexpected repairs. The children may need school clothing. Even Christmas, the celebration of the Lord's birthday, can hinder giving to God.

God understands there is never a convenient time for giving. That is why He gave us the following instructions.

> He that observeth the wind shall not sow; and
> he that regardeth the clouds shall not reap.
> In the morning sow thy seed, and in the eve-
> ning withhold not thine hand: for thou knowest not
> whether shall prosper, either this or that, or whether
> they both shall be alike good.
>
> **Ecclesiastes 11:4, 6**

There it is. The farmer who observes the adverse circumstances of nature will never plant his seed. There is never a perfect day for sowing. This same principle applies to the Christian who plans to give a significant financial gift to God. You must press on, even though it is not a convenient season.

Isaac had to disregard every adverse condition to obey God in sowing. When he sowed, in Genesis 26, the entire nation was in a death grip of drought and famine. Not only was the weather bad for sowing, but his wells had been stopped up by the Philistines. By faith, he paid no attention to these bad circumstances. He simply obeyed God and sowed.

There was no natural reason to justify the release of his precious seed into that parched earth. No man with good sense was wasting his seed on that hardened ground.

But Isaac had more than good sense to go on. He had more sense than the heathen did, for they had only five senses. Isaac had a sixth sense — faith in his God. Even in his seemingly impossible circumstances, Isaac's faith held on to God's Word. No matter how futile it seemed, he planted anyway. He did not plant in desperation, but he planted in faith. He had faith in God's instructions.

> **Then Isaac sowed in that land, and received in the same year an hundredfold: and the Lord blessed him.**
> **And the man waxed great, and went forward, and grew until he became very great:**
> **For he had possession of flocks, and possession of herds, and great store of servants: and the Philistines envied him.**
> **Genesis 26:12-14**

There is no reason to think this will not work for you. Isaac served the same God you serve today. He has not changed.

> ... I am the Lord, I change not ....
> **Malachi 3:6**

Jesus, our Savior, has not changed!

> **Jesus Christ the same yesterday, and today, and for ever.**
> **Hebrews 13:8**

Isaac operated under the same covenant promises in which you operate today. He was the seed of Abraham even as you are the seed of Abraham.

> **... If ye be Christ's, then are ye Abraham's seed, and heirs according to the promise.**
> **Galatians 3:29**

Remember, the promises to Abraham's seed include the power to get wealth.

> **... Thou shalt remember the Lord thy God: for it is he that giveth thee power to get wealth, that he may establish his covenant which he sware unto thy fathers, as it is this day.**
> **Deuteronomy 8:18**

The wealth of this promise can come from many places. However, the power to get it is activated when you plant your financial seed to a financial harvest.

> **Give, and it shall be given unto you; good measure, pressed down, and shaken together, and running over, shall men give into your bosom. For with the same measure that ye mete withal it shall be measured to you again.**
> **Luke 6:38**

Go Through This Process Step by Step

Allow me, once again, to take you step by step through God's simple laws of the harvest. Let this review prepare you to plant your seed to your own financial harvest.

Check off each step of the process as you agree to comply.

1. *You must plant a seed.*

Decide today that you *must* prepare an amount of money to give to the Lord. Do not worry at this moment to which ministry you will give. What is important now is that you decide you are going to give a specified amount of money (your seed) into the Gospel.

I understand this is not the most convenient time to give. We have seen that there will never be a convenient time. Resolve in your spirit that this is the day you will commit to give a substantial amount of money to God.

Remember, you are not planting your finances just to get rid of some money or help some preacher or project. You are deliberately giving your finances for the purpose of receiving multiplied finances back again.

Make a clear commitment to yourself and your God that you are giving this money with the full intention of following all the laws of the harvest.

_____ Yes, I will plant a seed.
_____ No, I will not plant a seed.

If your answer is no, go no further. Return to chapter one and start reading this book again. You have missed something. If your answer is yes, proceed to step two.

2. *When you plant your seed, it must become useless to you.*

Do not expect a harvest if you plant a seed that you do not allow to die. The seed (money) you plant must become useless to you.

Remember! There is a trend among some ministries to induce people to give by selling something to their partners. I am not saying it is wrong to buy or sell something. Just don't get confused into thinking this is giving to God, for it is not. If you purchase something, it is not the same as planting a seed. Buying products or privileges is not giving to God. This kind of ministry funding will not bring forth a harvest (multiplication) of funds.

I am not saying if you give to a ministry that sends you a gift in return that you have not allowed your seed to die. A book, lapel pin, or plaque does not disqualify a donation. These things are gifts from the ministry you have supported. The Holy Spirit will give you unction as to what is acceptable in this matter.

_____ Yes, I will plant my seed in such a way that I receive no benefit from it other than my promised harvest. It will be a gift to God with no strings attached.

_____ No, I will not plant my seed in such a way that I can receive no benefit from it.

If your answer is no, go no further. Return to chapter three and read it again. If your answer is yes, proceed to step three.

3. *You must plant what you desire to reap.*

If you plant tomatoes, you will have a tomato harvest. If you plant apples, you will have an apple harvest. If you plant afghans, you will have an afghan harvest. If you plant kindness, you will receive a harvest of kindness.

If you plant money, you will have a money harvest.

_____ Yes, the seed I am planting is a money seed. I am planting money expecting to reap a money harvest.

_____No, the seed I plant will not be a money seed, but I still expect to reap a money harvest.

If your answer is no, go back to chapter four and read it again. You missed the whole point of that chapter. If your answer is yes, proceed to number four.

4. *You must decide the size harvest you desire on the day you sow.*

This can be one of the most frustrating laws of the harvest to comply with. It is difficult to decide how much seed to plant. Please let me give you a Scripture and a brief comment.

The Apostle Paul helped the Corinthians with this problem.

> **For if there be first a willing mind, it is
> accepted according to that a man hath, and not
> according to that he hath not.**
> **II Corinthians 8:12**

If you have come this far, you have already decided to plant a seed. You are already of *a willing mind.* Next, the verse says the amount of your offering should be in accordance with your sufficiency, not your insufficiency. The amount you give should be decided by the size blessing God has given you, not according to the shortage you are experiencing.

When you plant a seed, there will be a natural tendency to decrease the size of your gift because of things you still need. Your offering should not be reduced because you have needs. It should be given in accordance with the blessings you can count. Don't penalize God because of the shortages you are suffering from the kingdom of darkness. Don't let your lack set the amount of your gift. Let God's abundant blessings set the amount.

> **Every one must make up his own mind as to
> how much he should give . . . .**
> **II Corinthians 9:7 *TLB***

You must make up your own mind how much to give. It will not be decided for you. You must remember, the size of the gift you give will decide the size of the harvest you reap.

> **... If you give little, you will get little. A
> farmer who plants just a few seeds will get only a
> small crop, but if he plants much, he will reap much.**
> **II Corinthians 9:6 *TLB***

The amount of your gift should be decided by the peace God brings to your heart.

> **... let the peace of God rule in
> your hearts ... .**
> **Colossians 3:15**

Let God's peace be the umpire when deciding how much to give.

_____Yes, I have peace about a certain amount. That amount is $_____ .

_____ No, I cannot decide how much to plant.

If your answer is no, stop here. Count your blessings and pray until God gives you peace about a certain amount. If your answer is yes, and you have written the amount down, proceed to step five.

5. *Your seed must be planted in good ground.*

You may want to reread chapter six to refresh your memory on how to choose a good-ground ministry for your gift. Put the ministry that comes to your mind to the simple tests we learned in that chapter. Remember to give great consideration to your local church if you know it is good ground. Make your decision under the supervision and guidance of the Holy Spirit, allowing Him a free hand to guide you in your choice.

I have taught you all I know in this matter!

_____ Yes, I have decided which ministry I will give to. It is:

Name _____

Address _____

Proceed to step number six.

6. *You must be ready to patiently wait until your harvest is ripe.*

_____Yes, I will patiently wait until the time of harvest has come. I will not cancel my harvest by growing impatient and slipping into unbelief. I will guard the words of my mouth.

Proceed to number seven.

7. *You must properly maintain your Christian life to experience a proper harvest.*

_____ Yes, I will faithfully tithe to keep the windows of heaven open so the seed I plant can properly grow.

_____Yes, I will live a godly life and seek first the Kingdom of God and His righteousness, so I will qualify to receive *all these things* that will be added to me.

If you answer yes, proceed to number eight.

8. You must sow to your harvest size, not from your harvest size.

Review step number four. If you do not have peace that the amount you decided to give is enough, increase it.

_____Yes, I am satisfied with the amount I am going to plant and it will be enough to meet my need in the harvest.

_____No, I am not satisfied with the amount of seed I planned to plant. I realize it will not be enough to meet my need at the time of harvest. I am increasing my seed to $ ____ .

Move on to number nine.

9. I am ready to make a special harvest-release offering when my harvest is ripe.

Please review chapter ten if you need to refresh your memory on this point.

_____Yes, I believe God has told me the proper amount to give to break my harvest from the stalk. It is $ _____ . I will give it when God says my harvest is ripe.

Continue to step ten.

10. You must be committed to plant again from your harvest.

_____Yes, I will sow again from the harvest I reap. Proceed to step eleven.

11. You must decide that a part of every harvest is for you to keep, without guilt.

_____ Yes, I believe that it is all right for me to experience a blessing from my coming harvest. I will not feel condemnation from receiving it, and I will enjoy purchasing the things I need and desire.

12. You must pray over your planted seed.

If you are to have a successful harvest, you must know it is God who is working the miracle of multiplication. It is very important that you pray regularly so your seed will multiply. Without fail, you must also put unbelief aside. Strong faith is needed for the release of your financial harvest.

> **And he did not many mighty works there because of their unbelief.**
> **Matthew 13:58**

_____ Yes, I have complete faith in God to give me a harvest.

_____ Yes, I will guard my lips. I will not speak words of doubt. If unbelief comes to my mind, I will not speak it, but I will cast it down as an evil imagination.

_____ Yes, I will pray regularly to God, the Lord of the harvest, that my harvest will come forth.

With all these steps completed, you are now ready to fill in the *sowing and reaping covenant*. Upon signing it, please send it along with your check to the ministry to which God has directed you.

A Covenant of Sowing and Reaping

Dear _____:

(Name of Ministry)

After prayerful consideration, God has led me to plant my financial gift in your ministry. A book I read about planting in good ground helped me choose your ministry.

I will be giving you $ _____. It will be given as follows:

_____ *In Full.* Check for the above amount is enclosed.

_____ *Faith Promise.* I will give you $_____.

per___week for ___weeks
per___ month for ___ months.

Please agree to pray with me that I will receive an abundant harvest from this gift to your ministry. I want to establish a relationship with you in giving and receiving like the Apostle Paul had with the church at Philippi. (Phil. 4:15.)

I expect you to faithfully pray for my harvest.

Sincerely,

Name _____

Address_____

City_____

State_____

Zip_____ Phone ( )_____

This covenant of sowing and reaping is from a book entitled *Hundredfold*, by John Avanzini, P.O. Box 1057, Hurst, Texas 76053.

168

15
Manifesting Your
Hundredfold Increase

**(I came) . . . not with enticing words of man's
wisdom, but in demonstration of the Spirit and of
power.   I Corinthians 2:4**

God wants to reveal Himself to you in the miracle of the
hundredfold financial increase. This is probably the boldest
statement I have ever made in print. I am declaring God's
desire to manifest Himself in your finances in this manner
because of the extraordinary way in which He revealed it to
me.

The things I am about to share with you came to me
during my most personal experience with God to date. To
reveal these things in print is the last thing I ever thought I
would do. The first fourteen chapters of this book were
already written when God impressed me to add this closing
chapter.

I advise you to be certain you have the leading of the
Holy Spirit before you act on anything written here. *If you act
on the things in this chapter without His direction, it will not
bring forth an increase.*

If you are to fully understand the signs and wonders God
is performing through my ministry, I must share something
that took place about ten years ago. It happened on the
continent of Africa, in the nation of Nigeria.

I am convinced that one of the reasons the Holy Spirit has led me to write this chapter is my recent visit to Nigeria. My spirit is always stirred when I go back to that nation. My journeys there are among the most exciting I ever take, for it was in Nigeria that God appeared to me in a supernatural way.

I have experienced several manifestations of God's presence during my life. However, I must say none has been as dramatic as was that visit. I went to Africa at the invitation of an international evangelist. I was asked to help him teach in a great school of ministry. This school had more than a thousand African ministers in attendance.

I arrived at the meeting a day late. It was on a Tuesday, and that day's session was already in progress. The building was full. Even its small balcony was jammed to overflowing.

As I entered the side door, I was impacted by the overwhelming presence of God. It was as if a great heat was emanating from the room. When I felt it, I immediately stepped back outside. As I considered what it was, I realized it was the warm glow of the Holy Spirit. Suddenly I knew what was meant when international evangelists described the Holy Spirit as "warm, liquid fire."

His presence was everywhere. The very air was filled with the anticipation of the people.

Not long after re-entering the room, a second speaker was introduced. As he spoke, the same presence filled the room. With each word, the people's faith grew. Suddenly, I realized that in an atmosphere like that, nothing would be impossible.

When the speaker closed his dynamic teaching, I was called to the pulpit and introduced to the people. I had previously been told I was allocated two hours to teach. This would be the first of four, two-hour sessions I would be teaching in that meeting.

No sooner had I begun to speak than the presence of the Holy Spirit lifted from the room. All I could hear was my own voice laboriously speaking. The words of my neatly prepared lesson notes were hollow sounding to say the least.

Now, don't misunderstand me. I was delivering great information to the people. But it was information that was void of any real *power!*

The faces in the congregation were now noticeably changed. The look of anticipation they all had a few moments earlier was now a look of disappointment. Where had the power gone? Where was the electrifying presence of God?

I spoke for what seemed to me to have been at least two hours. When I looked at my watch though, only fifteen minutes had passed! Worse than that, the second hand was still moving. It had not stopped running. I still had an unbelievable one and three-quarters of an hour left to speak.

Every cell in my body knew I would never be able to last that long. And even worse, I knew that under no circumstances could my audience last that long.

Finally, when half an hour had passed, I excused myself from the pulpit. I explained that my long journey had left me totally exhausted. I promised I would be back the next day, filled with new energy and the abundant power of the Holy Spirit. When I left the platform, the only sigh of relief louder than my own came from the congregation.

I had to face the ugly facts. I was out of place among the speakers on the program. They each possessed a power from God that I did not have.

Throughout my previous eighteen years of ministry, I had never before been confronted with anything like this. I had always preached and taught with a strong style. I had never "bombed out" before in my life, but "bomb out" I did. My teaching was a complete "bust."

As I went to my room, the words of my host rang in my ears. I vividly remembered the conversation that had taken place between us just two years earlier. I had asked him to allow me to accompany him to the foreign field someday to assist with the teaching. At the time, his reply had seemed very strange to me.

"John, anyone who goes with me to the foreign field, *must have a breakthrough ministry!"*

I immediately asked, "What is a breakthrough ministry?" He asked one of his associates to explain it to me. This kind brother began to tell me of the absolute necessity for the presence of the Holy Spirit when teaching in third-world nations. He explained that in most of these countries, our sessions would be the only formal training our students would ever receive. Because of this, it would be essential for the Holy Spirit to confirm the things that were taught with signs and wonders. If this didn't happen, my teaching would be of no value to them.

I must confess, I believed both the evangelist and his associate were trying to impress me with their spirituality. I was confident that my great preaching and teaching skills would be just as effective as theirs.

Two years earlier, their words had seemed like an exaggeration. That night as I sat in my dirty room, in a less-than-fine hotel, I understood perfectly what they had tried to tell me.

Here I was in Nigeria with my request answered. I was on the teaching staff with this great evangelist, but I was powerless.

We had all preached the Gospel that day. They had preached with the power and demonstration of the Holy Spirit, while I had only given out Bible information. They had shaken the place with their words. The only thing I had shaken was my confidence.

Needless to say, my first night in Africa was a living hell. Try as I might, I could not fall asleep. I was in a land that was ten time zones earlier than my hometown, but it was not jet lag that was keeping me awake. I could not sleep because my spirit was out of its comfort zone. I knew the truth. My preaching was void of God's power.

That night I repented, I prayed, I tossed and turned. Nothing helped relieve my heart's pain. I prayed for God's power. I prayed I would be miraculously released from the responsibility of teaching the next day. I prayed to go home. I prayed I would disappear. Foolishly, I even prayed that I would get sick and die. As the sun began to rise that Wednesday morning, I was aware of my spiritual bankruptcy as never before.

Without exaggeration, I can say the only teaching I have ever done that was worse than my teaching on that first day was my teaching on the second day. To say it stank would be a compliment.

Although I bombed out again, something inside me changed. I did not leave the platform in despair that second day. I left it with determination. I had an inner conviction that I would have power with God the next time I stepped back into that pulpit.

Once again, I went directly from the auditorium to my room. I immediately fell to the dirty floor and began praying with all my might. Again and again, I approached God's throne. "Oh, God! Give me a breakthrough ministry! I must have signs and wonders following the words you have given me."

I will always remember the name of that hotel in Abba, Nigeria. The Crystal Park Hotel is forever branded in my memory. It was neither grand nor prestigious, but it was the place where God visited me. It was the place where He endued my message of biblical economics with *power*.

As I prayed, suddenly something outside the scope of my experience began to happen. God manifested Himself to me *visibly!* Out of a bright, concentrated light He began to speak audibly to me. He said He had heard my prayer. He told me He was going to give me the breakthrough ministry I had asked for. However, this promise would be conditional. The condition would be that I would have to strictly obey Him in the operation of this gift.

I quickly answered, "Yes, Lord. I will do whatever you tell me to do."

Immediately He told me He had set me apart for the purpose of bringing the end-time message of biblical economics to the church. He promised He would be giving me many other startling revelations. From that day on, I would teach a very special end-time message. At the end of my session the next day, I was to take an offering. He promised He would miraculously reveal Himself through this offering with *unmistakable signs and wonders.*

The next words I heard came out of my own mouth. They totally shocked me. I said, "But, God, my host said there would be no offering taken until the day after tomorrow!"

What a strange thing for me to say to God, especially after I had just promised to explicitly obey Him. Now here I was arguing with Him. I was greatly impressed with the fact that He did not become angry with me. He simply repeated His previous instructions.

"John, if you want to have a breakthrough ministry with signs and wonders following, *you must obey Me.*"

I said, "Oh, God, please forgive me. I will do exactly as you say."

Immediately, He totally and completely forgave me. It was as if I had never even protested. I knew in my heart that not only had He forgiven me, but He had forgotten I had ever argued with Him.

He went on to reveal a truth to me that was almost unknown in the earth. At first it sounded unscriptural to me. He said, "I usually am not able to multiply back to My children the money they give to Me."

I asked, *"Why not God?* Throughout your Word you say you will."

"John, I know My Word says I will, but I can only do so when My people *give correctly.* I cannot multiply anything back to them that they have given improperly.

"My people usually make two great mistakes when they give to Me. First, they seldom give the *exact amount I tell them to give.* John, tell My people *I cannot multiply back to them that which they give to Me in disobedience.* If I did that, *My action would sanction disobedience."*

Then He said something I was not ready for. He said, "My people often *give more* than I tell them to give. After I tell them how much to give, sometimes the person taking the offering will *put undue pressure on them.* This sometimes causes them to disobey Me and give more than I told them. When I tell My children how much to give, they should never increase that amount *because of pressure.* Raising the amount because of pressure is an act of disobedience to My Word. It is giving preference to the words of the man who is putting them under pressure instead of giving preference to the words I have spoken."

He went on to explain that His people *can* give more than He instructs them to give if they do so out of love for Him. He is always greatly blessed by people who give this way. They are the people He referred to when He said *He loves cheerful givers.* (II Cor. 9:7.)

He said, "There is a *second* thing My people do when they give that stops Me from giving back to them. Most of the time they give to Me without desiring a specific result from Me. They are not expecting anything from their gift. John, the multiplication of money back to the giver is *always* accomplished by *a miracle.* All miracles operate by *faith.* When My people give without a desired result in mind, *they do not give in faith.*"

He then quoted to me from Hebrews 11:1, "Now faith is the substance of things hoped for. . . . It is impossible to give to Me in faith *unless you are hoping for something from Me in return.*"

"Tell My people they must always follow these two important steps when they give. *First,* they must always give the amount I tell them to give. *Second,* they must give it with full expectation of receiving it back from Me multiplied. *Every gift must be given in obedience and faith.*"

The next thing God said to me has proven to be the most phenomenal thing in my ministry. It is greater than I can even comprehend. I literally stand humbled before God by the immense power of it. I always give Him all the glory, for it is totally beyond my own abilities.

He said, "I am going to attach signs and wonders to your ministry. I will do this as long as you preach My Word and strictly obey Me. These great signs and wonders will begin tomorrow. When you teach the people these *two principles,* you will also allow everyone who will *obey them* to give in the special offering I have instructed you to receive. Clearly direct anyone who cannot be obedient *not to give anything."*

"Those who feel they qualify to participate in this special offering *must agree to one more thing.* They must believe with you, that when you lay your hands on the offering, *it will be multiplied* back to them *one hundredfold.*

"The prayer you will speak while you lay your hands on the money *must not be a long prayer.* Just speak that the offering before you will be multiplied one hundredfold. Speak this prayer in the name of Jesus. *That is your only part in the miracle. My part will be* to miraculously multiply back a *one hundredfold increase* to those who obey."

"When you have prayed, *do not be discouraged* by those who say they did not receive the hundredfold increase. Only I know who has given in *obedience* and in *faith.* Carefully look and listen, for there will be *many who will receive* the hundredfold. It will be the *obedient ones* who will encourage you."

With that said, the presence of God began to leave the room. Once again I cried out uncontrollably, "God! *Can't we wait* to do this at a time when I am in front of a smaller crowd of people?"

Without arguing, He answered, "John, *I will be multiplying the money, not you.* I can save one or one million with the same word. *My words are creative words.* Just go and do as I said. I will do the rest."

As the light of His presence left the room, I could see that dawn had once again come to the city of Abba, Nigeria. It was Thursday, my third day in Africa, but it was a significantly different day. This was the first day of God's new, breakthrough, miracle anointing on my ministry.

On my way to the teaching session, I was nervous, to say the least. My host had clearly said there was to be no offering taken that day. But my God had said there would be one taken. He had made it clear that it would not be just another offering. It would be a very special one.

These thoughts of the offering were not my only source of anxiety as I rode to the meeting. I had to face the continuing pressure that awaited me at every intersection along the route. The car assigned to drive me back and forth was on its last leg. Nothing on it seemed to work, not even the brakes. Each time we came to a stop sign, my driver would have to rebuke the oncoming traffic. Miraculously, we had arrived safely each day. Now, on this special day, there seemed to be a close encounter at every intersection. By the grace of God, we made it to the meeting without incident.

I entered the building and stepped up to the pulpit. My appearance before the crowd brought no great anticipation to their faces. But as I began to speak, they quickly changed. It was immediately evident that there was a new anointing upon me. Each word of my message was filled with power. The air began to fill with the presence of God. It was absolutely wonderful. In that moment, I promised myself I would never again stand before any congregation without this power. I had drunk from the cup of God, and the new wine was wonderful!

As I began to conclude my message, the high praises of God were upon everyone's lips. Then I made the announcement. I told them God had instructed me to take a special offering that morning. Immediately, a hush fell over the audience. All eyes turned to the host evangelist. Everyone was waiting to see his reaction! He stood to his feet and said, "John, if God told you to take a special offering, go ahead and take the offering!"

There it was! God had clearly borne witness to the man of God! With his approval given, I quickly told them who would be allowed to give in this offering. I explained the two great hindrances that were keeping the Lord from multiplying their previous offerings back to them.

When I was sure everyone understood the two requirements for proper giving, I told them there would be a miraculous manifestation of the one hundredfold increase to everyone who would join their faith with mine in this meeting. I rehearsed to them that I would lay my hands on the offering and speak the few words God had instructed. I clearly told them this miracle would come to everyone who would give in *obedience and faith.*

The ushers had barely started collecting, when the offering containers were full. This caused a brief moment of confusion among the ushers. What a miracle! Ninety percent of the congregation had not yet given, and the offering plates were full and overflowing.

Then, an enterprising young African solved the problem by going to the dormitory and getting two pillowcases. Enthusiasm began to grow. Row after row of excited donors placed their money into the offering. After what seemed too long, the ushers finally came forward with the two pillowcases almost full to the top. I couldn't believe what I was seeing! They were used to only filling soup-bowl sized offering plates, but under the anointed teaching, they had filled two pillowcases!

I asked everyone to rise and extend their hands toward the offering. As I opened my mouth and began to pray, a loud voice cried, *"Wait! Don't pray!"*

You cannot imagine the thoughts that ran through my mind. I just knew a terrible thing was about to happen. To my left, I saw a man moving quickly toward me. I thought, "Oh, no. He must want his money back!"

But instead of asking me to return his money, he wanted to put more money into the bag. He began to empty his pockets saying, "I almost did not give the amount God told me to give."

Why, I had never in all my life seen anything like this. Someone actually stopped the offering so he could put in more money!

Once again, we bowed our heads to pray. As soon as my eyes were closed, I heard another voice cry out. *"Wait! Don't pray!"* Each time I tried to pray, more and more people came forward crying, *"Don't pray! I haven't given what God told me to give!"*

Finally, the evangelist rose to his feet and extended both hands toward the congregation. He said, *"Stop the giving!"*

In all the years of my ministry, I had never heard of anyone giving the order to stop an offering. I had only read of it in the Bible.

I glanced at my watch and noticed that over an hour had passed since I first started to pray. Both pillowcases were now jammed to capacity with money. Watches, rings, money, and articles of clothing were ankle deep on the floor around me. I closed my eyes and said, *"Be multiplied one hundredfold in the name of Jesus"*.

As I walked away, the joy of the previous moments was instantly snatched from me. The presence of the Holy Spirit lifted just as quickly as it had come. All I could feel was the horrible presence of evil all around me. My ride back to the hotel was a half- conscious experience. Brakes failed, accidents almost happened, but I was unaware of the events of our journey.

The devil had come to sift me. He was lashing out foul accusations. He told me I was a failure, and the evangelist would never again invite me to go anywhere with him. He said I had tricked the people into giving more than they should. He told me many of them would have to go without food, lodging, or transportation. He repeatedly accused me of being a charlatan and an exploiter of the innocent. He convinced me that I had given them nothing more than false hope. I was defeated. All I could pray was that God would quickly take me out of Africa.

The morning light found me still awake, wishing I was home. I answered the knock on my door that Friday morning with dread. I did not want to face that congregation again. Reluctantly, I opened the door, expecting the worst. Instead, I saw my driver standing there with a broad smile on his face. His only words to me were, *"Come, see!"*

As I followed him down to the front door of the hotel, I must honestly say I did not want to see anything else in Nigeria. All I really wanted to see was my home back in the United States.

When we came to the parking area, my driver led me to a brand new car. I looked at it and spontaneously said, "Thank God, they finally got us a decent car to ride in!"

Then my driver said, "Brother John. You don't under-stand. God gave me this car last night. It is mine! It is *my hundredfold return!* It happened just as you prayed it would."

My faith immediately skyrocketed! The miracle of the hundredfold blessing had actually happened to this man in less than twenty-four hours!

On the way to the meeting, he eagerly told me of the previous night's visit to his lost uncle's house. The uncle was a very rich man. Before that visit, he had never shown any interest in his nephew. However, that night *things were different*. After a wonderful evening of fellowship, his uncle totally surprised him by giving him the new car. It was an absolute gift, with no strings attached. The wealth of that unsaved uncle was miraculously transferred into the hands of that child of God. It had happened just as God had told me it would.

Before that year was over, my Nigerian driver and his family came to the U.S.A. He stood before the church I pastored and gave personal testimony of his hundredfold increase. He also brought with him a list of the names of many other Nigerians who had received the miracle of the hundredfold increase from that meeting.

Since that great day in Africa, I have ministered this miracle increase offering in churches across America. It has also been demonstrated in Canada, England, South Africa, Kenya, Brazil and Asia. It has been witnessed by thousands through national television. Every time this message is spoken, the results are the same. Many are miraculously blessed with the hundredfold increase. The churches where I share this increase always invite me back to speak again. I meet people in airports, at conventions, and on the street who say they have received the hundredfold increase. Everywhere, the report is the same. *Praise the Lord, it works!*

It is always interesting to see the different amounts God tells people to give. One person in Florida was told to give $20,000. A man from Los Angeles gave $10,000. A businessman from the Philippines gave $100,000. Many give $1,000. This seems to be a very common amount. Some folks give

$5.00 or $10.00. The amounts vary greatly, but, from person to person I hear the same thing again and again. "It works. We received the one-hundredfold increase."

As I said earlier, I was hesitant to write this chapter. Even as I started, I felt it was too personal to put into print. I felt it would be too easily misunderstood. Then, halfway through writing it, I received a phone call. I couldn't believe my ears when I heard who was on the other end of the line. It was my driver from Nigeria. He was the first man who ever experienced the hundredfold increase when I laid my hands on his offering. He said he was on a short visit to the U.S.A. and felt impressed to call and say, "Hello." While he was on the phone, we talked about the miracle automobile he had received.

When I hung up the phone, I knew God was telling me the time was right to put the miracle of the hundredfold increase in writing.

In closing this book, I must say again that this great miracle sign and wonder does not come forth by my own power. I give God all the glory each time it happens. I simply obey Him, laying my hands on the offering and speaking the few words He has instructed me to say.

As always, I stress to the giver not to feel any pressure to give *more* or *less* than God says to give. This is very important. Some people have told me that they gave less than the amount God told them to give, and *absolutely nothing happened.*

The people who report the hundredfold increase to me

always confirm they did two things. First, they gave the amount God told them to give. Second, they stood in faith, without wavering, believing God for an increase.

Since writing this chapter, I have instructed my staff that every letter that comes to my office asking for the miracle prayer of the hundredfold increase *must* come to my desk for *me to personally lay my hands on.* I have stressed to them that *I must speak the one-hundredfold increase over each individual letter.*

Now that this book is complete, I wish each of you a great increase as you implement the laws of the harvest I have taught you. No matter where God leads you to sow, I will faithfully pray with you for your abundant harvest. When you receive it, please write and let me know the details. Tell me where you planted, how much you gave, and how much you received back from God. Let me know how long you waited for your return. Include any other details.

I await word of your greatly increased harvest!

John Avanzini was born in Paramaribo, Surinam, South America, in 1936. He was raised and educated in Texas, and received his doctorate in philosophy from Baptist Christian University, Shreveport, Louisiana. Dr. Avanzini now resides with his wife, Pat, in Fort Worth, Texas, where he is the Director of His Image Ministries.

Dr. Avanzini's television program, *Principles of Biblical Economics*, is aired five times per day, seven days per week, by more than 550 television stations from coast to coast. He speaks nationally and internationally in conferences and seminars every week. His tape and book ministry is worldwide, and many of his vibrant teachings are now available in tape and book form.

Dr. Avanzini is an extraordinary teacher of the Word of God, bringing forth many of the present truths that God is using in these days to prepare the Body of Christ for His triumphant return.

To contact Dr. Avanzini, write:

John Avanzini
P.O. Box 1057
Hurst, Texas 76053

*Please include your prayer requests and
comments when you write.*

THE POWER PACK

FAITH EXTENDERS
Everyday Ways To Increase Your Faith $8.00

BIBLICAL ECONOMICS IN COMICS
(Lockman) $7.00

STOLEN PROPERTY RETURNED
Or The Law of Retribution $6.00

ALWAYS ABOUNDING
The Way To Prosper In Good Times,
Bad Times, Any Time $6.00

FIVE TAPES
Seven Ways of Receiving From God $7.00
How To Get God's Attention $7.00
Reaping In Your Recession $7.00
Why God Prospers His Children $7.00
Lessons In Tithing From Genesis $7.00

TOTAL BOOKSTORE COST $62.00
SPECIAL OFFER #1
ONLY $30.00

FOUNDATION PACK

POWERFUL PRINCIPLES *(One Book)* $9.00
THREE TAPE SERIES
Giving, Receiving & God's Abundance (ea $8.00) $24.00

TOTAL BOOKSTORE COST $33.00
SPECIAL OFFER #2
ONLY $25.00

(ADDITIONAL OFFER ON OTHER SIDE)

WEALTH TRANSFER SYSTEM

THE WEALTH OF THE WORLD *(One Book)*
Yours For The Taking $7.00
THREE TAPE SERIES
Wealth Transfer System (ea. $8.00) $24.00

TOTAL BOOKSTORE COST $31.00
SPECIAL OFFER #3
ONLY $25.00

PURCHASE
ALL THREE SPECIAL OFFERS
FOR ONLY $70.00

IN ADDITION, Brother John wants you to
RECEIVE A GIFT OF A VIDEO TAPE entitled
"WAS JESUS POOR?"

PLEASE SEND ME:
- ☐ OFFER # 1 @ $30.00
- ☐ OFFER # 2 @ $25.00
- ☐ OFFER # 3 @ $25.00
- ☐ ALL THREE OFFERS, PLUS VIDEO @ $70.00
- ☐ VIDEO TAPE ONLY @ $30.00

NAME _____

ADDRESS _____

CITY _____ STATE _____ ZIP ....

PHONE (_____) _____

☐ *CHECK*　　☐ *MONEY ORDER*　　☐ *VISA*　　☐ *MASTER CARD*

CARD # _____ DATE OF EXPIRATION _____

MAIL TO: HIS IMAGE MINISTRIES　BOX 1057　Hurst, Texas U.S.A. 76053
(817) 485-2962